the PILLAR B's

The Pillar B's
How to Transform from your Biggest Critic to your Best Coach

ISBN 979-8-9874132-0-3

©2023 by Ray Santiago III

First Edition

The names and sports of the persons described in this book have been changed
or altered to maintain confidentiality but the stories are true.

Editor: Mike Yorkey, MikeYorkey.com

Cover Design/Interior Layout: Emily Muse Morelli, www.bluemusestudio.com

the
PILLAR
B's

How to Transform from your
Biggest Critic to your Best Coach

RAY SANTIAGO III

Dedicated to my wife, Mindy

A special thanks to:
Heather Palmer-Caldwell, Mike Rolls,
Mike and Laurie Kaminski, J.K. Mondol, Steve Holley,
and Donnie & Sheri Abeloe who each gave me
the opportunity to fall in love with sports.

CONTENTS

INTRODUCTION

by Ray Santiago III

In the summer of 2019, the Houston Astros posted a position opening for a mental performance coach. I applied, and two weeks later, I received an email from their sports psychology department requesting a preliminary video interview.

I was ecstatic to say the least. It was always my dream to make it to the Major Leagues. When it didn't happen as a player, I held out hope I could make it as a mental performance coach. This was my chance.

On interview day, I cleaned my room, put on a collared shirt, positioned my computer with the best lighting I could manage, and took a few deep breaths to calm the nerves. The interview process would be an hour-long Q&A. No interviewer. Just a distracting video of my face, a question on the screen, three minutes to answer, and my future on the line.

I settled into my seat and just before I clicked start, my mouth became a desert, my heart raced, my body shook, and my mind went blank as a whiteboard. Good thing my future wasn't at stake.

Instead of clicking start, I guzzled a glass of water and lay on the ground. With my eyes closed, I brought my awareness to my breath until my heart slowed and my body relaxed. Then, I smiled as I imagined rocking the interview and answering each question with confidence and clarity. After a few more deep breaths, I sat up. With eyes still closed, I allowed face after face to filter through of all the athletes I'd helped to believe in themselves one play at a time.

That's all I needed. I was convinced. I was ready. There wasn't a person in the world I trusted more than me at that moment to nail the interview and work with the Houston Astros organization. Cocky? No. Confident? Absolutely. With the resumé to back it up. When was the last time you believed you were the best in the world to get the job done in the moment?

I sat back down in my chair, took a few cleansing breaths, smiled, and clicked start with my chest out and chin up. Question by question, the blank whiteboard in my mind filled with solid answer after answer.

Cruise control. Not thinking. Just speaking.

Perhaps you've felt that. Not thinking. Just playing. Everything goes as desired, and you can do no wrong.

That was me for almost an hour straight until—just like in every game we've played—something goes wrong, like making an error or missing a crucial shot. For me, it was a question my mental whiteboard had no answer for: "What framework do you use when working with athletes?"

Framework? Sure, I learned the theories in graduate school, but after I put the textbooks away, I thought I had graduated to modeling what the best sports psychology professionals in the industry were doing with real clients: breathing exercises, positive self-talk, emotion management, and routines. *What did I need a framework for?*

I tried to save face by throwing out a few names and theories I vaguely remembered, but I would've been better off staring blankly at the camera for three minutes with a bead of sweat trickling down my face. Needless to say, I didn't get the job. I didn't even get a second interview. I'll never know if it was due to that question or something else. But I didn't let that setback discourage me. I used it to set up my next move. If a professional sports organization thought that question was important enough to ask, I knew I better have a good answer for it the next time an opportunity to work with the best athletes in the world arose.

This book, *The Pillar B's*, is that answer. Too late for the interview. But perfect timing for you.

What the Houston Astros were asking me was this: when an athlete comes to you for help, what's your approach? Somehow, I'd never asked myself that question. If I was going to be effective in helping athletes with their mental game, I needed a framework on paper to help them pinpoint their problems *and* provide a game plan to help them regain and maintain their confidence.

I wasn't trying to reinvent the wheel, so I researched what was already out there. It didn't take me long to come across Cognitive Behavioral Theory (CBT), a common framework used throughout psychology to help people struggling with confidence, anxiety, and depression, among other issues. In short, CBT says this:

Your thoughts impact your feelings.

Your feelings impact your physiology, or body.

Combined, your behavior—what you do—depends on your thoughts, emotions, and body sensations.

Light bulb.

My framework had been CBT all along. I just didn't know it. Nor was I using it properly. As an athlete, your performance results from your thoughts, feelings, and physiology.

My mission was to simplify the psychology into a language athletes could understand and apply quickly. Hence, the **Pillar B's** are:

- **Believing** (thoughts): The chief cornerstone of your confidence. Before, during, and after competition, your believing will be tested.

- **Breathing** (emotions): Control your breathing, and you'll control your emotions. Otherwise, your emotions will control you.

- **Body** (physiology): The mind and body are one. Where your mind goes, your body follows.

- **Battling** (behavior): Your actual performance that everyone sees.

On every play, what you **believe** influences how you breathe. How you **breathe** tells the **body** it's ready or rattled, which ultimately dictates how you **battle**. The strength of your Pillar B's will determine whether you withstand or wither under the pressure of competition. You can leave your performance to chance or change your strategy to control what's in your control. Your Pillar B's are in your control.

Here's the Pillar B framework that has helped countless athletes make sense of their struggles and point them back to success—all in less than an hour session.

That doesn't mean everything's fixed in an hour. Hence the *I-N-G Principle*. You'll notice three of the four Pillar B's end in *ing*: believ*ing*, breath*ing*, and battl*ing*. In the English language, adding *ing* to a verb makes it an ongoing action in the present moment.

It's not enough to believe in yourself for one play. What happens when you make a mistake, get pulled, or fall behind early?

Anyone can take one deep breath. But what happens when your heart and thoughts start racing when under pressure?

Controlling your body is easy when going well. But what happens when you tighten up after an error, or when you see a lake and sand trap surrounding the green?

Anyone can compete for one play. But what happens when the other team has the momentum? What if your greatest opponent is *you*?

Sports never go perfectly, so there must be a constant re-upping of your Pillar B's. Who's responsible for that constant reset? You are. Every. Single. Play.

Finally, in the middle of the Pillar B framework, you'll see the words *what, where, who,* and *when*. There's a background story to every performance problem. Maybe it's the pressure of a championship game. Securing a scholarship. Worrying about the draft. Making Dad proud. Or interviewing for a dream job. This background noise directly impacts how you think, feel, and perform. With the Pillar B framework, you'll be able to reframe the background noise, so the moment works for you rather than against you.

You love your sport. You're good at your sport. But sports are hard and you are human. Now you have the answer to any performance problem holding you back from playing your best. It's time to unpack the Pillar B framework. Let's start with the background story behind the thoughts, feelings, and body sensations causing you to play less than your best.

Scan the QR code below to instantly download your FREE Pillar B's Handbook that complements each chapter and receive BONUS audios for breathing exercises and visualizations.

1

TEEING OFF

In the spring of 2021, a French golfer named Victor Perez prepared to tee off at the World Golf Championships in Austin, Texas. After five grueling days of one-on-one match play, only eighteen holes against Matt Kuchar stood between Perez and a third-place finish. To most professionals, finishing third is finishing short. But on this particular Sunday, a third-place finish would be as sweet as winning it all.

What was at stake?

Beating Matt Kuchar would bring national pride to France, secure Perez a PGA Tour Card (guaranteeing him tour exemption for at least a year), boost his FedEx Cup Leader Board standing, and earn him $740,000 in prize money. Might there have been a little background noise competing for Victor Perez's mental real estate as he prepared to tee off?

Think about some of your best and worst performances. They weren't random. Background noise pushed you to play at your peak or detoured you towards disaster. Understanding how background noise affects your Pillar B's will help you discover the pressures you may be under and how they impact your thoughts, emotions, body, and, ultimately, your performance.

Back to Victor Perez.

In the tee box of the first hole, Perez could remember that he was one of the best golfers in the world (believing) and steady his heart rate with deep performance breaths (breathing). Those calming breaths could relax his grip (body) and allow him to smash his opening drive (battling). Or he could let the background noise pressures and expectations overwhelm his confidence, accelerate his heart rate, tighten his grip, and burst his ability to drive the golf ball.

The result of his tee shot? An uncharacteristic hook into the trees. Matt Kuchar had also hit into the trees nearby. Perez had a decision to make. He could take the safe approach, knowing he had up to seventeen more holes to battle, or force a risky shot to reach the green.

Perez chose risky and overshot the green, landing out-of-bounds. Even after a penalty stroke, he still could've tied the hole by safely chipping up onto the green. But he attempted another tough shot to land near the flag stick, came up short, and watched his ball roll back out-of-bounds.

There's a good chance Victor Perez allowed the background noise to hinder his ability to control his confidence, emotions, body, and game plan, which ultimately cost him the match and all that came with it. What about you? Are you aware of how your background noise negatively impacts your Pillar B's?

THE FOUR W'S OF THE SPORTS BACKGROUND

The four W's of every sports background are: what, who, when, and where. Building an awareness of the story running in the background of your performance will help minimize outside noise so you can see game situations as they truly are—not worse.

WHAT

Moments in sports get their meaning from *what's at stake*. At Gonzaga's first fall practice of the 2020-2021 basketball season, their record was

0-0. By the national championship game against Baylor, they were a perfect 31-0. Leading up to the championship, the media discussed whether Gonzaga could finish off their perfect season and finally get the monkey off their backs of never winning the big one.

Might the stakes have been a little higher than that first fall practice? The mind and body are quite aware of the magnitude of the moment, even if you keep telling yourself it's just another game.

Based on past experience, consider how your Pillar B's are impacted by what's at stake. Using a pen, rate yourself on the following (1 = not a lot at stake to 5 = a lot at stake).

____ Playing in the backyard

____ Practice

____ Tryouts

____ Opening day

____ Regular season game

____ Showcase tournament

____ Playoffs

____ Championship game or series

WHO

Are you more worried about the opinions of who's watching than what's happening in the game? How does who's watching and who's competing influence your Pillar B's?

Rate your comfort level playing in front of the following (1 = very comfortable to 5 = very uncomfortable):

____ Mom

____ Dad

____ Siblings

____ Significant other

____ Close friends

____ Coaches

____ Teammates

____ Scouts or college recruiters

____ Good competition

____ Particular umpires or referees

____ Large crowd

____ Small crowd

WHEN

Everyone struggles at different times and under different circumstances. Rate yourself on a scale of 1-5 on the following: (1 = rarely struggle and 5 = almost always struggle).

____ Beginning of game

____ End of game

____ After success

____ After failure

____ Practice

____ When people expect you to perform well

____ Regular season

____ Playoffs

____ Championships

____ Night games

____ Day games

WHERE

Certain places cause you to perform well or not so well. A golfer playing at a course he's played well at in the past tends to feel confident going into his next round there. A different golfer who played poorly at the same course last time out might be less confident going into her next round.

Your events can take place just about anywhere at any time. Are you aware of how your Pillar B's are impacted by different locations under various conditions?

With the following, rate yourself on a scale (1 = rarely struggle to 5 = almost always struggle).

____ Home game

____ Away game

____ Humidity

____ Heat

____ Good past experience

____ Bad past experience

____ Travel more than three hours

Now you have a greater awareness of how your background noise will try to attack your Pillar B's. Circumstances are ever-changing. But how you view your circumstances can remain steady.

The rest of this book will equip you to withstand the noise that's competing for a spot in your mental locker room, and the first place the sports background will attack is your believing. Let's solidify your confidence one thought at a time.

Pillar 1
BELIEVING

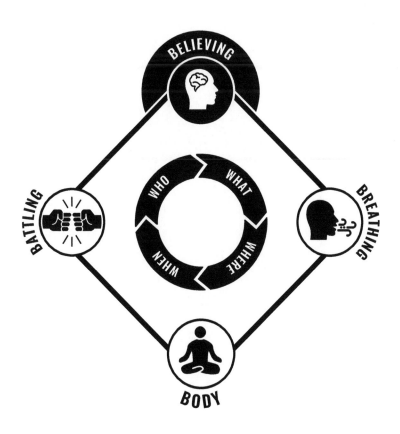

INTRODUCTION TO THE BELIEVING PILLAR

"You have to have the mental resilience, toughness, and discipline to believe in a shot you haven't hit yet, even after hitting a bad shot."

—Thane Ringler, former pro golfer, on Grant Parr's 90% Mental Podcast (episode 147)

Your believing will be challenged every moment of your athletic career. As someone who teaches the Pillar B's and strives to live them, I still struggle to believe in myself consistently. During the writing of this Believing section, I went to the local practice range to experiment with believing in myself with each golf swing. I purchased the 115-ball bucket, which gave me 115 opportunities to be fully persuaded beyond a shadow of a doubt that I could hit my desired target. Hitting the target wasn't as important as believing I could do it. Believing you'll do what you're setting out to do is the first step in consistent high-level performance.

The next day, I asked several of my mental game clients, "Out of the 115 swings, how many do you think I successfully believed that I would hit my target?"

Some said 115 out of 115. I laughed. *They have more faith in me than me!* Another said 100 out of 115. Someone else sheepishly threw out fifty. Still not close. I could honestly admit to fully believing in my swing on about 35 of the 115 balls. That's about 30 percent of the time.

Why is it so hard to believe in ourselves? The battle for believing is a two-front war between external distractions (through our five senses) and our inner demons (our thoughts and emotions). A basketball player can see a huge defender and feel threatened (external) or a golfer could recall (internal) missing three straight putts and lose confidence. To win the battle of believing, you must be able to see what's really there (external) and choose to perform confidently (internal) despite how you may feel in the moment.

On the practice range that day with my 115-ball bucket, the *external* distractions I allowed to hinder my believing included: unpleasant weather, neighboring chatter, and the golf mat I stood on. Some *internal* distractions included: personal expectations, achy body, comparisons, frustration, success, failure, boredom, fatigue, mechanics, negative self-talk, and anger. You might understand now how I could only believe in about 30 percent of the balls I hit.

I learned something valuable that day. If you can believe in yourself for just one moment, it must be possible to repeat it. The more you repeat that steady belief, the better you'll play. You only ever have this moment. And the next. When you string enough *this* moments together, it ends up being an entire round of golf, a basketball game, a lacrosse match, or a career.

Difficult? Yes. But so is playing from fear which is far less enjoyable. Being an athlete is a tough pursuit, so why would the mental process be easy? Stay strong. You'll see improvement in your game quickly as you fortify your believing.

The only promises competition ensures are chance, change, and challenge. From your very first play until your last, adversity will be like a best friend who sticks by your side, ready to make you better if you allow it. That's why confidence, or *believing*, is the most important pillar to master. Your thoughts—where your believing stems from—give meaning to situations, which pump life into your emotions, which grant orders to your body, which sets in motion your performance—all for good or bad.

You can give your believing away, but no one can steal it. You must protect it. What will test your believing? Everything. Yourself, the opponent, teammates, coaches, fans, weather, and the game situation. Desire to be tested. Gold is refined by being put to the fire. When you're put to the test and pass, you'll be refined in mind and body. Stronger. Mature. Battle-tested. Ready for anything.

There are five sections in the **Believing Pillar** to help you rubberize your confidence to help you bounce back from any adversity:

- **Pure Perspective:** Seeing what's actually there—not better or worse
- **Identity:** Knowing who you are, why you play, and how you prepare
- **Self-Compassion:** Showing up for yourself no matter what
- **Vocabulary of Victory:** Speaking powerfully to yourself and others
- **Vision:** Experiencing victory before it happens

Section I

PERSPECTIVE

2

ABOVE ALL ELSE . . . BELIEVE YOU'RE THE BEST

"I never lose. A guy might strike me out, but I got myself out . . . Just always staying in the positive lane at all times and believing you're the best. When I step on that field, I know I'm the best. I believe I'm the best. It's just a matter of continuing to work."

—Tim Anderson, Chicago White Sox shortstop

In 2006, baseball's Houston Astros held a tryout in Venezuela for sixty prospects. Among them was a scrawny sixteen-year-old billed as a can't-miss prospect. Except he was the wrong kind of can't-miss prospect. Despite his obvious talent, 5-foot, 6-inch, 140-pound Jose Altuvé looked more like a high school freshman than a professional baseball player. With several MLB organizations having already written him off due to his size, the Astros were his last chance.

Being labeled "too small" was nothing new for Altuvé. He'd heard it his entire life. Yet, he refused to believe his size should dictate his future. On day one of the tryout, he put his skills on full display. Of the sixty prospects invited, only twenty-five received a callback for day two, but Altuvé wasn't one of them.

To his credit and boldness, he showed up the next day hoping for another shot. In attendance was Al Pedrique, a native Venezuelan and the Houston Astros representative at the time. Flight troubles had delayed him from attending day one, where he'd hoped to scout Jose Altuvé based on a recommendation. So, with Pedrique vouching for him, Altuvé was given another chance and didn't disappoint.

Pedrique later recounted, "The way he swung the bat, how he handled himself on the field, the energy. Altuvé was different compared to everybody else. The way he walked on the field, handled himself, how quick his hands were. He ran the 60 yards and was the fastest guy in the group."

Beyond his talent, what separated Altuvé was the way he carried himself. In other words, his believing. To him, he belonged on that field and was the best prospect available. *That's* believing despite the circumstances.

After the tryout, an ecstatic Jose Altuvé signed a contract for $15,000, and by 2011 was the Houston Astros' second basemen. In 2012, he was an All-Star. From 2014-2018, he finished in the top thirteen in American League Most Valuable Player voting, despite being the shortest player in the MLB. In 2017, he edged out Aaron Judge (the tallest position player in the league) to win the AL's MVP award.

If Altuvé hadn't believed he could become one of the best professional baseball players in the world, he wouldn't have shown up for the second day of tryouts after being told to go home. He wouldn't have played in front of Al Pedrique, who signed him. And, he wouldn't still be wreaking havoc on my New York Yankees.

Your ability to believe in yourself with little supporting evidence is a true mark of mental maturity and crucial if you plan to take confident action in pursuit of your dreams. So, above all else, believe you're the best.

Is it easy? It wasn't for Jose Altuvé and won't be for you. Every day, on every play, you'll be challenged to prove you belong. Embrace it. No one's going to believe in you until you first believe in yourself.

In 2017, when Altuvé won the American League Most Valuable Player award, the baseball world finally validated what he alone believed way back in 2006 on that dusty field in Venezuela—that he was the best in the world. It all starts with the power of believing.

Now, on to building yours.

Within minutes of meeting new clients, I share that I only work with the best athletes in the world. Usually, their faces say, *You've got the wrong athlete.* I repeat, "I only work with the best athletes in the world."

Still not knowing what to do, they laugh awkwardly and avoid eye contact. I smile, and repeat myself, following with, "I want you to walk out the door. Take as much time as you need. But when you return, choose to believe you're the best."

Now it's your turn.

Take a few deep breaths and envision some of the greatest moments in your career, where for even one moment you were the best. Then, believe it by allowing that moment to travel south from your head to your heart. When you believe you're the best, it's like an eagle wanting to burst out of your chest. Practice this enough, develop the work ethic to back it up, and you've got a bucket full of believing on speed dial.

The main point of the *best in the world* exercise is to demonstrate that confidence is first a choice before a feeling. Some athletes aren't ready to believe in themselves or just haven't been taught how. If that's you, it's okay. This Believing Pillar will teach you to crave those moments.

For the athletes who return through my office door ready to believe in themself, they enter beaming with their chests out and chins up. They may feel a little uncomfortable, just like you might, but it's due to trying on the "best in the world" mindset for the first time. Firsts can be a bit awkward, but this mindset is worth getting used to and the only one that'll get you where you want to go.

If you think you need success or some special feeling to be confident, those may never come. Anyone can be confident when they're playing well. But can you bank on your believing after a mistake? Two mistakes? After being benched? You can when you make confidence a choice. Mature believing means you can call on confidence no matter how you're playing.

What you choose to believe about yourself heavily dictates how far you'll go in sport and life. If you're okay with being mediocre, then mediocrity is what your body will demand of you. If you expect to become elite, there seems to be two choices:

1. Believe you're the best.

2. Believe something else.

Don't be fooled. There's really only one right choice. Believe you're the best. Every. Single. Play. But let me offer this disclaimer. Although it sounds like it, believing you're the best doesn't concern itself with comparisons. It doesn't mean you think you're better than anyone else. It doesn't require you to have the most talent. It also doesn't presume you're blind to other good players around you. **Believing you're the best means you're fully persuaded you will get the job done right now.**

You won't find a better mindset. Again, it may be uncomfortable at first. But it needs to become your norm. Others may feel uncomfortable around such confidence. That's their problem. They have the same privilege and opportunity as you to develop a strong self-belief backed up by proper preparation. Make the most of the time you have by making the most of the mind you have. Be the best in the world in your mind.

If only one can win, believe it's going to be you. What's the worst that can happen? You fail? You risk failing every time you play. If you're fortunate to play long enough, you'll lose often and make plenty of mistakes. That's sports. True satisfaction comes from winning in your thinking. If you approach each situation with full believing, that's a win. Desired results will follow.

Do you struggle to recall concrete proof demonstrating for even one play, you were the best? That's okay. Who do you admire in your sport? Mimic them until you have some personal victories. Pretending to play like someone else still forces you to believe in yourself. Even with no prior success, it's still possible to believe you are the best in the moment.

At the time of this writing, my wife and I had just welcomed a baby boy into the world. I'd never held a baby, let alone changed a diaper. How did I build my confidence in something I'd never done? I studied the nurses changing my son's diapers. When we returned home from the hospital and it was dirty-diaper time, I took a deep breath (away from the diaper), smiled, and repeated, "I'm the best diaper changer in the world. Best diaper changer in the world."

My first effort wasn't perfect, but it went really well. My hands responded to the confident mindset I'd developed from watching the best diaper changers in the world at the hospital. By diaper thirty, there was still plenty of room for improvement, but by then I had some success to lean on.

Can you watch Mike Trout? Alex Morgan? LeBron? Nelly Korda? Mimic their believing until it becomes yours.

What's the difference between *thinking* you're the best and *being* the best? A powerful example comes from the late Heath Ledger, who famously locked himself in a London hotel for a month studying comic books and previous Batman shows and movies for his upcoming role in *The Dark Knight* as the Joker. Ledger's family later revealed that Ledger told them it was the most mentally and physically draining experience of his career. But, by the end of his preparation, he wasn't just acting—he *was* the Joker.

Despite the example's overshadowing darkness due to Heath Ledger's death (ruled as an accidental prescription drug overdose), it's a true testament of an A-List actor fully embodying his role both mentally and physically. Practicing. Rehearsing. Becoming.

Have you fully committed to being who you need to be in your sport?

Do you set aside time for watching or imagining highlight reels of your greatest moments to become the best rather than just play the part?

Being the best in your own mind will have a far greater impact on your performance than simply thinking you're the best. You won't always get the results you desire, but ideal results will consistently come when you become the best in your mind. When you make a commitment to being the best, it must be a commitment to both mental and physical development.

Since the best in the world know confidence must first be a choice, let's practice again: Think back to some of your top performances. It could be yesterday or five years ago. Pick one in particular. Go there. Smell the smells, feel the feels, fully experience everything. Capture the moment. Live it out in HD. Now, take a few deep belly breaths (inhale belly rises, exhale belly falls). Close your eyes and replay a particular moment several times while declaring, "Best in the world . . . best in the world . . ."

How do you feel? If it's cheesy at first, stick with it. You'd rather feel cheesy and be the best than feel cool and be retired. Once you've captured the feeling of being the best, it's yours to experience anytime you want.

Why is it often easier to believe in teammates or opponents more than in yourself? Perhaps you give others too much credit based on their size, talent, past performances, or national ranking without having an intimate knowledge of their inner demons. You're all too familiar with yours, so you discount your abilities while forgetting that underneath a few layers of athleticism, other athletes are imperfect humans, too. Other athletes likely have as many fears and doubts as you. Stop giving others too much credit and start giving yourself proper credit.

The fact that your opponent is also human should bolster your believing. Each performance then comes down to who's going to control his mind, emotions, body, and game plan better. Unless your opponent is training her mind to think the best, you already have the advantage. The mind dictates performance. If your mind is weak, your body is weak. Often, your opponent is only one or two chips away from cracking.

By making the time to read, highlight, and scribble notes throughout this book, you're putting in valuable work at the mental gym to become the best in the world in your thinking. The mental gym is almost always empty. Advantage you. Few ever make the time to build their mind. Coincidently, few ever become the best.

Believing you're the best doesn't mean you'll always win. It just means you'll rarely beat yourself. The following list shows what the best in the world *do not* always do:

- Win.
- Start.
- Come through in the clutch.
- Think the right thoughts.
- Believe in themselves.
- Play perfectly.
- Have fun.
- Treat others well.
- Give or have 100 percent effort.
- Stay healthy.

What *do* the best in the world consistently do?

- Study losses and mistakes to grow.
- Prepare like a starter and anticipate their moment to shine.
- Strive to win and never give up. Michael Jordan said, "I never lost. I just ran out of time."
- Welcome pressure moments.
- Catch themselves thinking negatives and reframe them quickly.
- Know they are humans trying to accomplish super-human tasks.

- Mess up. Make errors. Fall short. Have fears and doubts. But consistently find a reason to believe in themself despite the circumstances.

- Don't just hope to succeed . . . they expect to.

- Give 100 percent of what they have. Sometimes that's 75 percent. But they give 100 percent of that 75 percent.

- Treat injury rehab like it's their career.

I've received pushback from some athletes about the "best in the world" thinking, citing there's no way they could ever be the best. I say, "You don't have to be the best all the time. Just in moments. No one else better. Right here. Right now."

Now, I invite you to set the same standard of believing. Close this book and don't open it until you *choose* to believe you are the best at what you do. Take your time. See it in your mind. Feel it in your bones. After that, the hardest part is over until an internal or external adversary tries to dethrone your believing. The challenges will come quick. Every day. Anticipate them. Welcome them. The battle of believing is the only one you're guaranteed to win if you don't give in. Your enemies, like fear, pressure, anxiety, and perfectionism are coming for you. Good. You'll be ready.

Tackle each challenge with joy because each obstacle will be an opportunity to strengthen your believing. A weightlifter can't get stronger without lifting heavier weights. You can't get mentally stronger without overcoming adversity. No need to fear. This book will be your spotter.

Next, we'll set up a security system to keep out any external voices persuading you to believe anything other than being the best. Since believing happens in the mind, that's exactly where the opponent will target. Let's protect it.

3

SECURING YOUR
MENTAL LOCKER ROOM

Every professional stadium has a "Players Locker Room" door that athletes dream of entering someday. Protecting that entrance is a security guard who denies access to anyone without proper credentials.

Throughout my childhood, my dad took me to Angel Stadium in Anaheim, California, to watch baseball games. When the Yankees were in town, we waited outside the Players Locker Room in hopes of getting an autograph or at least a glimpse of our baseball heroes. I'll never forget seeing Yankee shortstop Derek Jeter walking next to his manager, Joe Torre, on their way to the team bus. Seeing them further fueled my dream to play Major League Baseball.

As I got older and experienced better competition, it became clear how difficult it would be to gain access to the Players Locker Room one day. As you know or will soon find out, the sports world is a pyramid—not a sphere. Way less than one percent of athletes earn access to the Players Locker Room.

When it comes to your thoughts, research shows you have anywhere from thousands to hundreds of thousands of thoughts per day. That's a lot of inner dialogue to contend with, especially on top of input from social media, YouTube, TV, friends, family, coaches, and teammates, etc.

It's interesting how we protect our cars and homes with locks, and our phones and computers with passwords, yet, how much unquestioned access into our minds do we allow the world's negativity?

Juliet, a client of mine, received a phone call from a "friend" the night before their teams faced off in a championship game. This girl told Juliet that her squad was going to beat Juliet's team and that she had told her teammates all of Juliet's tendencies and weaknesses to shut her down.

Some friend, huh? Juliet was understandably shaken. It was proof she needed to establish a mental security guard. Personally, I would've hung up on that girl.

Have you set up a mental security guard to protect your mental locker room? Or does every random thought, critical voice, social media post, or crazy idea have free access to your inner self? If you ever expect to belong in a professional Players Locker Room, make it your highest priority to develop a strong mental security guard who only allows entrance to elite thoughts. Anything less than the best can join the rest—outside.

Why is protecting your thought life so important? Your thoughts dictate how you feel, and how you feel dictates how you perform. Basically, the quality of your performance depends on the quality of your thoughts. Remember: everyone wants to take down the best, but they can't get what they can't get at. So, protect your mind. Your believing is at stake.

By limiting access to only thoughts and ideas that improve the way you think, feel, and play, you create a winning culture inside your mind. You can't control what comes knocking, but you can control what you let in. What you let in and what you kick out is up to you. Few things in your career will be totally in your control, but your mental locker room is one of them.

In *Man in the Arena*, a documentary about Tom Brady's career, Tom spoke about "ignoring the noise." Part of what made the New England Patriots great during the Brady years was their hard-nosed stance on blocking out any drama infiltrating their locker room and causing division. They understood division creates distrust. Distrust creates doubt. Doubt drains confidence.

No more was this apparent than in the 2014-2015 playoffs when the "Deflategate" scandal broke out regarding the use of under-pressurized footballs.[1] Anyone looking to bring down the Patriots found their fuel.

The Patriots' response? Within their locker room, they simply determined to ignore the noise and focus on their next game—Super Bowl XLIX against the Seattle Seahawks, which they won.

After the season, the Patriots were handed a $1 million fine, lost two draft picks, and Tom Brady was suspended for the first four games of the 2015-2016 regular season. Brady and the NFL Players Association fought the suspension throughout the season but lost his appeal before the start of the 2016-2017 season.

When Brady returned, the Pats were 2-2. Doubts of the dynasty flooded ESPN and social media. The Patriots ignored the noise again and embarked on another Super Bowl season, coming from behind 28-3 to beat the Atlanta Falcons 34-28 in Super Bowl LI. New England didn't use words to fight back. They spoke with their performance.

No one can argue with winning. The Patriots' incredible comeback was a microcosm of the comeback they had made all year from the Deflategate scandal hovering over them. Each player first made the commitment in their own minds to ignore the noise. Then, collectively as a group. That's how you dominate for twenty years.

In sports, believing you're the best option for the situation is the healthiest perspective and greatest blueprint for battle. Very few will ever believe you're the best. Everything in the sports world will try to persuade you that at best—you're second best. That's why you must protect your mental locker room if you plan to excel.

List the external noise that currently has access to your mental

---

1 Brady was alleged to order the deliberate deflation of footballs. Removing air from a football makes it easier to grip, throw, and catch.

locker room. What level of focus will you have once you mentally clean house? When you keep the best and constantly kick out the rest, all that will remain are your best thoughts. That's when believing you're the best becomes easier.

Listen, I know it's hard enough to keep the negatives out. It's even harder when the negatives are already established veterans living in your mental locker room. The next chapter focuses on the self-limiting beliefs seeking to corrupt your mental locker room culture if they're not kicked out and replaced.

4

CENTRAL BELIEFS

Imagine five hats on your kitchen table representing different college scholarship offers. As you pace back and forth, weighing the pros and cons of each one, your five-year-old cousin says you should play for the team with the red hat.

Would you let him decide your future? It might be entertaining to listen, but you wouldn't put your future in a five-year-old's hands, would you?

It might surprise you to learn that most of your current thoughts, emotions, and behaviors while performing are based on beliefs you established in youth sports. What you saw on the field, heard from coaches, and experienced during games helped establish your beliefs about yourself, other players, and where you fit into the sports world. Those beliefs can be so deeply ingrained that you've never thought to question them—until now, I hope.

Unless you pause to examine your current beliefs for accuracy, your younger you will continue running or ruining the show. What's at stake? Everything. Your beliefs dictate how you think, feel, and perform. If your beliefs are warped, everything else will be too. Here's an example of how beliefs established early on can impact a career if they're not addressed and changed.

SARA'S SELF-LIMITING BELIEFS

Sara and I started working together on her physical and mental game before her high school freshman soccer season. She wasn't the most physically gifted, but her work ethic rivaled my top athletes. When it came to giving herself credit after a grueling workout, however, she'd brush it off as no big deal. Similarly, with preseason goal setting, instead of reaching for lofty but achievable goals, she'd find a way to sell herself short, saying things like, "Oh, you know, I just want to make the team."

She gave the same answer before her sophomore and junior seasons. Why was she putting in so much work just to sell herself so short? Her self-limiting beliefs were feeding her lies, and she was eating them. When Sara's senior season rolled around, I wasn't about to let her accept her "just happy to be here" speech again. She was capable of more.

So, before a particular workout, we went on a walk, and I asked her an important question. The answer held the key to unlocking a door she'd accidentally closed on herself long ago. A door that you have likely locked on yourself in at least one category of sports or life.

"Sara?" I asked. "When did you form your beliefs about yourself as an athlete?"

Only the crunch of early autumn leaves underfoot could fight the silence. With an uneasy smile, she responded, "I was always the fat girl on my teams growing up."

She let those words walk with us for a moment before continuing. "And the fat girl is always the slowest. I've never considered myself fast or super athletic. Those are obviously important things in soccer, so I've never expected to be one of the best on the team or anything."

Bingo.

I turned to her. "You do realize you're not that girl from pee-wee soccer anymore, right?"

Sara had transformed her body over summer break after her sophomore year to get faster. By tryouts junior season, she was an athletic specimen. She had changed physically. But mentally, she was still the unathletic girl from youth soccer.

Back to our walk.

"I know I'm not the fat girl anymore," she continued. "But I thought losing all that weight would make me faster. But it didn't."

"Do you have any proof that you *are* faster?"

"Okay, to this day, I don't know how it happened, but last year [her junior year], at conditioning, the varsity coach had the JV and varsity teams line up for sprints. Somehow I finished in the top five. I seriously don't know how that happened. Everyone must have been running slow or something."

"Or?"

"No. I'm seriously not that fast. Everyone on my team is always like, 'Sara, you're fast. Why don't you believe us?'"

"Yeah, Sara. Why don't you believe them?"

"Because I've never been the fast girl."

"Okay." I stopped my stride and turned to her. "I think you grasp you're not that little girl anymore, but I don't think you realize she's still running the show."

With that realization, Sara had to decide whether to remain shackled to her self-limiting beliefs or break free and form new beliefs about what she was capable of doing. We all do.

Early in my baseball career, I was considered a good base stealer. Then, in an important game, I got picked off first base. After that, I was never aggressive when stealing second base. I let a single moment traumatize me and grow into a self-limiting belief that dictated how I performed as a base runner for the rest of my career. Did getting picked off one time make me a bad baserunner? No. But in my young mind at the time, that's how I saw it. I believed it.

What about you? Take a moment to consider any self-limiting beliefs you may have established at some point. It could've been in school when all the other kids finished their tests early while you were only halfway done. Was that when you believed you'd never be as smart as everyone else? To this day, do you still struggle to see yourself as intelligent compared to others? Are those limiting beliefs still true? Were they ever?

THE HEART BEHIND SELF-LIMITING BELIEFS

Here's what's interesting: Your self-limiting beliefs try to protect you. When you fall short, those feelings persuade you not to try too hard or get your hopes up again. They make you believe you're just not cut out for certain sports or school subjects. But even if those self-limiting beliefs were partially true back then, they're now holding you back from fully embracing who you are now and what you're striving to accomplish.

Those early experiences don't have to be the final say in how your sports career plays out. I've had athletes who never made an All-Star team go on to play at the Division 1-level because they refused to believe what their youth experiences seemed to show about where they stood.

Everyone's sports journey is different. What's not different is each athlete's ability to choose their beliefs. Beliefs might be formed in youth sports, but they're not hard-wired DNA. They're changeable.

What might've shaped your beliefs about yourself as an athlete for good or bad? If you had a rough youth sports experience, you may have developed a self-limiting belief system like Sara. But what happened back then doesn't have to dictate what happens now unless you let it. You're still one decision away from believing you're the best.

THE FOUR CORE NEEDS

Every human has four core needs: to be effective, loved, worthy, and safe. When our needs aren't met, we develop self-limiting beliefs to justify why. Most of our self-limiting beliefs stem from a sense of ineffectiveness (not being good enough), unlovability, unworthiness, and danger. It's worth noting that if you struggle with one or more of the following self-limiting beliefs, they may only show up when you're playing poorly. Also, if you suffer from depression, self-limiting beliefs can cloud your perspective to the point where there's no being talked out of them.

Let's take a closer look at these self-limiting beliefs:

Helplessness/Ineffectiveness

- "Everyone is so much bigger, stronger, faster, and more talented than me."
- "My team doesn't need me. I don't contribute anything positive."
- "What's the point in trying if I'm just a bench player?"

Unlovability

- "No one even cares that I'm here. I'm the team reject."
- "Everyone looks so much better in their uniforms than me."
- "No one will like me unless I play well."

Worthlessness

- "I always let my team down. I'm a letdown."
- "When I'm injured, it's like I'm invisible."
- "I don't deserve to be on this team with the way I play."

Danger

- "I'm going to get injured."
- "Every referee has it out for me."
- "Nothing ever goes right for me."

Do you relate to any of these? If so, how do these self-limiting beliefs influence your believing? If none of these sounds like you, it doesn't mean they don't exist. You might be unaware of them, or they may show up in other areas of your life. A good way to learn about your self-limiting beliefs is to monitor what you think, say, feel, and do when adversity strikes.

HOW SELF-LIMITING BELIEFS KILL CONFIDENCE

It's your birthday, and you run outside to find a brand-new basketball hoop fastened above your garage. Except, instead of a circular rim, it's square. You pick up a regulation-size basketball and take a few dribbles. You're pretty sure any shot will rim out, but you put up a few anyways. Sure enough, no matter how perfect the shot, the round ball gets rejected by the square rim.

This is what happens in your mind when you experience positive moments [round basketballs] that don't align with your self-limiting belief system [square hoop]. Even in the face of clear evidence [a perfect shot], you can still be quick to reject or ignore progress or good performances. On the flip side, you have no problem accepting negative performances [square basketballs] that align with your self-limiting beliefs, further cementing them as truth.

When I met Shawn in his sophomore year of high school, I quickly learned how much time he spent in the gym. Ever since middle school, coach after coach had told him he needed to get stronger if he ever wanted to wrestle in college. What Shawn didn't know was this: each coach's words fortified in him a self-limiting belief of *ineffectiveness*, as in "I'm not strong enough."

No wonder he became a gym rat.

When I taught Shawn about self-limiting beliefs, I asked him to present any evidence proving he *was* strong. After some thought, he shared that he must be getting stronger because he was in the gym almost every day [round basketball]. He'd been consistently hitting new personal bests in lifts [round basketball], and his muscles had finally filled out his XL practice shirts [round basketball].

How much of that positive evidence fit through his self-limiting belief system of *not being strong enough*? About as much as Sara's evidence that she was fast. You guessed it. None. Why? Because the positive evidence [round basketballs] didn't fit what Shawn believed about himself [square hoop].

Unfortunately, any negative experiences, like missing a new personal best [square basketball] fit through the hoop just fine and confirmed his belief that he wasn't strong enough. These were the "I told you so" experiences that fed into what Shawn already believed to be true about himself. Any positive experience trying to challenge Shawn's self-limiting beliefs got rejected. In this wrestler's mind, despite glaring evidence of his strength, he was still a scrawny seventh grader.

It's nearly impossible to develop a healthy self-image when you can't get past your past. There is a way positive experiences can fit through the square hoop, which is to disqualify them.

DISQUALIFYING THE POSITIVES

Athletes willing to acknowledge positives must still justify them to accept them as true. I call it, "Yeah, but" disease, or YBD for short. YBD requires positive or neutral experiences to be spun negatively before being accepted. Or said another way, round basketballs must become square to fit through the hoop.

For Sara, it was, "Yeah, I finished in the top five, but everyone must've been running slow."

For Shawn, the back-and-forth went like this:

"Shawn, your biceps are filling out your practice shirt nicely."

Shawn: "Yeah, but this shirt shrank in the dryer."

"You hit another personal best on the squat rack?"

Shawn: "Yeah, but all my teammates are still way stronger than me."

"Your speed and power are really showing on the field."

Shawn: "Yeah, but I don't have a scholarship to show for it."

Shawn disqualified every positive by twisting it into a negative. We often think of these athletes as "Debby Downers," but some athletes cannot accept or enjoy success when it's staring them in the face because their self-limiting beliefs blind them. YBD destroys any momentum towards greater confidence, self-worth, progress, or enjoyment of sport.

The baseball player who smashes a double into the gap and thinks, "Yeah, but if I were stronger, that would've been a home run," is taking a confidence-building moment and cheapening it to become further evidence of falling short.

How about the basketball player who scores fifteen points in the second half and gets praised in a post-game interview and responds, "Yeah, it was nice finding my shot. But I have no clue what was wrong with me in the first half." While there's an acknowledgment of the positive, there's a dwelling on the negative that discounts an incredible second half. Also, the failure became personal to this player. What's wrong with *me* is much different than what's wrong with *my shot*.

The possibility that this player is human and sometimes misses shots is overlooked when she believes she should be perfect. Despite her first-half struggles, she persevered and kept shooting in the second half, while other players may have shied away from the basket and looked to pass the ball to a teammate. This player couldn't appreciate that fact because her mind was focused on the first-half failures.

Your focus impacts your feel. Having fun is hard when you're consistently focused on your shortcomings. If it's hard for you to enjoy success because you believe your performance wasn't good enough or you aren't good enough, you're likely suffering from YBD and self-limiting beliefs. You may be forfeiting progress and pleasure by demanding perfection.

Here's what I'd like you to do: write down any self-limiting beliefs that might be causing you to reject, ignore, or disqualify positive evidence that you're good enough and decide whether or not they are true. If they're not true, consider throwing them out and focus on what is true.

SELF-LIBERATING BELIEFS

If you had a relatively positive youth sports experience and upbringing, with some failures mixed in, you've likely developed a healthy belief system, or what I'll call self-liberating beliefs.

Liberating means freeing, where you don't hold yourself back. A self-liberating belief system is available to any athlete at any time, no matter their past belief system. Self-liberating beliefs are the sweet spot that'll help you navigate your athletic career.

Self-liberating beliefs grant you the freedom to acknowledge that your life and career will be filled with ups and downs. Losses and gains. Successes and failures. Self-liberating beliefs provide an overall healthy perspective and optimism about the future.

As discussed previously, every athlete has four core needs: to be recognized as good at their sport (effectiveness), accepted by teammates and coaches (lovability), to feel connected to others (worthiness), and to feel safe (protection). When you get your needs met, you can establish self-liberating beliefs:

Effectiveness

- "I am good at my sport even when I'm not having my best game."
- "I consistently contribute to my team's success."
- "Compared to others, I measure up pretty well."

Lovability

- "Overall, I'm liked by my family, teammates, and coaches."
- "I'm comfortable with my uniqueness. Everyone has their strengths and weaknesses."
- "Even if I don't have my best game, my family, coaches, and teammates still care about me."

Worthiness

- ◆ "I know I'm not perfect. But no one is."
- ◆ "I know I'll have bad games and make mistakes. But I'm not a bad person or a mistake."
- ◆ "Even when I'm injured, I can still make a valuable contribution to the team."

External Safety

- ◆ "Every time I compete, there's a chance I get injured."
- ◆ "Certain teammates and coaches I can trust and others I probably can't."
- ◆ "Not everything will always go my way, but that's just sports."

Depending on your current beliefs, these self-liberating beliefs land somewhere between achievable and seemingly impossible. But they are possible. Self-liberating beliefs don't guarantee you're always going to be happy or perform well. They simply paint a realistic picture of the good, bad, and neutral times throughout your career.

HOW TO CHANGE YOUR BELIEFS

Remember, your current beliefs aren't your DNA. Thus, they're changeable. At a certain point in history, most believed the world was flat, and therefore, they didn't venture too far offshore in fear of falling off the face of the earth. When it was discovered that the world was round, explorers started setting sail for new land and adventure. A change in beliefs led to a change in behavior. What might a change in beliefs do for you?

If you realize self-limiting beliefs are holding you back and you have a desire to make a change, you've already completed **step one**: awareness. **Step two** involves bringing your current beliefs to the witness stand and asking, "Is what I believe actually true?"

If your self-limiting beliefs are telling you your mechanics must be perfect for you to play well, is it true? No. That's a lie and a threat to your performance. Self-liberating beliefs say, "I don't have to have my 'A' game to be effective. I can still win with my 'B' game."

Step three is accepting that your self-limiting beliefs are false and need replacing. Self-limiting beliefs give you one constraining option. Self-liberating beliefs give you the truth and creative alternatives. Leaning on what's actually true will help you reshape your basketball hoop from a square to a circle so that positives (round basketballs) fit through and help build your confidence. **Step four** is to repeat this process every time a self-limiting belief tries to uproot a self-liberating one.

Is it easy to follow these steps? No. Crucial? Absolutely. It's not about dismissing all negative experiences or thoughts like they don't exist. It's about accepting what happens (good and bad) without giving them more or less importance than they deserve. Being neutral allows you to own your mistakes, learn from them, and embrace what to do next. (I'll share more on this later.) That way, not everything will need to go your way for you to feel effective, loved, worthy, and safe.

Making the shift from limiting to liberating beliefs is a moment-by-moment choice that gets easier. But if you don't take the time now to uproot your self-limiting beliefs, they'll only plant themselves further and continue to distort your thoughts. Especially your automatic thoughts.

AUTOMATIC THOUGHTS

Automatic thoughts are exactly that—automatic. They come to you within milliseconds of encountering a situation. If these automatic thoughts are accurate, awesome. If not, they become automatic negative thoughts—or ANTS. And like ants, once you see one, you know there's bound to be more. The only way to beat your automatic thoughts to the punch is by changing the beliefs that dictate them.

When something negative happens but you've properly trained your mind, your first thought response could be, "That happened. New moment right here." This would be a direct reflection of a self-liberating belief system and the truth. After a mistake, saying, "You idiot, how could you do that?" is a direct reflection of a self-limiting belief system and a lie.

If you plan to become an elite athlete, look at your current beliefs and make sure they're lined up with where you're trying to take your life and career. In order to change your automatic thoughts, you must change your beliefs. Right believing leads to right thinking.

Athletes who are especially tied to their athletic identity ride the biggest belief rollercoaster of all. When things are going well, it's easy to believe you're the best. When things aren't going well, it's hard to believe you're talented at all. When athletes with self-limiting beliefs play below their abilities and get pulled from the game, they automatically internalize this as confirmation that they not only played terrible—they are terrible. How do you think they perform when put back in the game?

One of my basketball clients believes her first shot dictates what kind of shooting day she'll have. Another client believes he should get on base every time he comes to the plate. Both are pressure packed beliefs and lead to automatic negative thoughts.

Understand you are human. Sometimes you'll be hot, other times you'll be cold, or somewhere in the middle. When positive momentum occurs, ride it. But stop any potential downward momentum by reminding yourself the past doesn't have to dictate the now. What happened doesn't have to decide what happens next.

A great way to kill ANTS is to believe the facts. Not the fiction.

BELIEVE FACTS, NOT FICTION

Your mind will tell you stories. Facts will tell the truth. What's your shooting percentage? What does the stopwatch say? What's your typical golf score? These are the facts, and you tend to play to your averages. Use your numbers to boost you when they're in your favor. If you're playing better than your average numbers, enjoy the ride. Keep it simple. Overthinking how well you're playing is your quickest route to self-sabotage.

A client of mine at the Major League level learned from a teammate how to play to his strengths simply by studying the numbers. In 2020, the numbers revealed that not a single batter had gotten a hit off my client's four-seam fastball. He was shocked, mostly because he barely threw his four-seamer in the minor leagues. Yet, at the Major League level, it was his most effective pitch. Knowing the numbers—the facts— helped him develop confidence that his four-seam fastball not only worked, but it was his most dominant pitch. What do your numbers reveal about you?

DO YOU CONTROL YOUR BELIEFS?

Did you hear about the homeless man whose brother was a successful businessman? When asked why they turned out the way they did, they both answered, "My dad was a drunk."

No matter what has happened in your life (without downplaying any terrible experiences you've had to endure), you are in control of your beliefs. Remember: your genetics and upbringing are outside your control. But you're not doomed by your DNA or upbringing. Right now, if you choose, you can decide which belief system you want to go with that will set the course for your future. Self-liberating or self-limiting? Which will you choose?

The choice is simple but not necessarily easy. The length of time any self-limiting beliefs have been spreading roots in your mind will determine how much time and effort it'll take to uproot them and replant liberating beliefs. Whatever you need to do, do it. The enjoyment of life and sports depends on it.

In the next chapter, you'll learn about cognitive distortions. These are the lies your self-limiting beliefs have sold you over the years. If your beliefs are skewed, the way you interpret game situations will be too.

5

THE LIES WE BELIEVE

Some athletes crave pressure-packed moments. Others pucker up. Some players crumble after mistakes. Others rebound quickly.

Same situations. Varied responses. Why? Because athletes view their competitive world through a unique set of lenses shaped by their beliefs. Lenses with the wrong prescription, called cognitive distortions, spin a skewed version of the truth rather than the truth itself. If you plan on believing you're the best in the league, the city, the state, the country, or the world, it's paramount that you start seeing each moment as it truly is—not worse. Below are common cognitive distortions that skew your perception of reality and how to fix them.

+ **All-or-Nothing Lenses:** Late New York Yankees owner, George Steinbrenner, liked to pump his fist and shout, "Anything short of a championship is failure!"

 Is that true? No. But all-or-nothing athletes think in terms of "I had the worst game" with no positives or "I had the best game" with nothing to improve. Since failure occurs more frequently than success, athletes wearing all-or-nothing lenses ride an exhausting emotional roller coaster that is an absolute confidence killer.

- **Removing All-or-Nothing Lenses:** Every game isn't good or bad. Every game is good *and* bad. "Good" and "bad" are the extreme ends of the performance spectrum, with plenty of gray areas in the middle for learning and improvement.

  Live in the gray. That's where growth happens.

  A client of mine during his high school baseball tryout, lined out to the shortstop in his first at-bat and struck out in his second. He believed he blew the tryout. After we talked, he realized coaches would rather see a guy line out than reach base on a swinging bunt. He also recalled how he maintained positive body language after striking out, showing coaches he could remain confident even after failure.

  Living in the gray area restores your believing and helps you maintain a healthy perspective of small victories amidst failure. All-or-nothing lenses are blind to the gray area of improvement. Choose to live in the gray where growth and motivation thrive.

- **Over-Generalization Lenses:** When these athletes struggle early, they believe their poor play will continue, and nothing will go their way.

- **Removing Over-Generalization Lenses:** Is it true one mistake guarantees future failure? No. So why destroy your own believing? Every performance is a series of moments. Your ability to compartmentalize your performance into airtight moments will allow you to keep the past from affecting the present and the present from predicting the future.

  Think of the bottom of a large cargo ship that is sectioned off into vast airtight compartments. If one compartment incurs water damage, the captain can seal it off. This way, a single hit doesn't bring down the entire ship. When adversity strikes, will you seal off mistakes so one miscue won't sink your entire performance?

  Mistakes and momentum shifts will happen. But one possession never defines an entire game. Rebound quickly with facts (fielding or shooting percentages) and forgiveness. It'll keep you from steering your performance into emotional wreckage. Nobody knows the pivotal moment in a game until it's over, so treat each new play like the pivotal moment.

- **Negative Filter Lenses:** These athletes focus on what they did wrong and filter out all the positives.

- **Removing Negative Filter Lenses:** When making macaroni and cheese, do you strain the pasta and keep the hot water? Of course not. But maybe you do this in sports when you hold onto your negatives and strain out all the positives. Some of my football clients sheepishly share that one dropped pass can block out all the nice catches they make. Focusing on a short list of negatives instead of an abundance of positives is a surefire way to lose confidence. Errors, dropped passes, and crucial missed shots are going to happen. When they do, fix them in your mind. Then move to the next play.

- **Labeling Lenses:** Players who label themselves or others tend to make snap judgments based on one or two negative experiences. A blown play becomes a personal attack rather than a chance to evaluate a play gone wrong.

- **Removing Labeling Lenses:** You are not your performance. A failed attempt doesn't make you a failure. Labeling yourself as a failure is personal and permanent, while labeling your attempt as having failed is performance-based and temporary. Believing you're a failure will cause you to put in less effort or give up. Believing you failed at one attempt will fuel your competitive drive and keep you hungry to try again.

- **Mislabeling Lenses:** These athletes prescribe over-the-top descriptions to their performance, a person, or teams, resulting in an amplified emotional reaction. Here are some examples:

    "That was a *terrible* putt."

    "He's the *worst* umpire in the league!"

    "My coach has *absolutely no clue* what she's doing."

- **Removing Mislabeling Lenses:** Keep the emotional coloring out of it. Was it really a *terrible* putt? Or was it just a missed putt? Is that umpire *really* the worst? Or is he a human being doing the best he can? Does your coach *really* have no clue what she's doing? Or are you mad about your current lack of playing time?

  Feeding your mind extremes like *worst, terrible,* and *absolutely no clue* is emotional firewood that will only burn your belief down. These extreme descriptions will dictate how you perform next if you let them. When your opinion is sometimes confirmed (an umpire you mislabel as terrible does make a bad call), it only fuels your feelings and further steals your focus, energy, and control. You'll either blow up at the umpire or be so mentally divided that you perform far below your capabilities. Instead, approach each moment with a neutral, open, or optimistic mindset so you finish the moment strong.

- **Personalization Lenses:** These athletes take coaching feedback as a personal attack, try to shoulder team losses, or think, "If it's meant to be, it's up to me."

- **Removing Personalization Lenses:** When it comes to constructive feedback from a coach, teammate, or scout, listen with an open mind. Someone sees something about your game and wants to help you improve. Act on what's helpful and throw out the rest. Worry when you're not receiving feedback.

  When your team loses, you may be tempted to believe a mistake you made caused your team to lose. It's not true. You are never the sole reason for a loss. Teams win or lose collectively, not individually.

  You are not the reason someone doesn't like you. You may have said or done something that he or she disliked, but each person chooses their attitude toward others. If you're a talented athlete, count on having haters. But keep your focus on how you can improve and help your team win. Let others be responsible for how they spend their energy and focus.

- **Magnification Lenses:** This athlete makes a bigger deal of things than is necessary.

- **Removing Magnification Lenses:** When a scientist observes cells under a microscope, do the cells actually grow? No. The cells are the same size. The microscope just magnifies them.

  It's hard to believe, but each game is truly just a game even though the pros say, "Everyone knows it's not just another game." To some extent, they're right, since what's at stake dictates how much pressure you feel. Yet, when everyone is settled into their seats for the Super Bowl coin toss, the game is still played one down at a time for four quarters.

  Let your opponent get emotionally caught up in the "big" moment while you keep things simple. Your sport is played with the same rules, whether it's a regular season game or a championship. Will you magnify the moment or see the game as it truly is?

- **Minimization Lenses:** This athlete downplays the significance or importance of something.

- **Removing Minimization Lenses:** I personally struggle with this one. After working on a novel for two years entitled *Playing on Higher Ground*, the book won a runner-up award in Young Adult Fiction. When I found out, I was happy for about five minutes. Then I was on to the next thing. Even if my book won first place, my response would've been similar.

  My wife encouraged me to pause and drink in the moment. She was right. It was worth acknowledging all the hard work that went into that book and the people I hoped it would benefit. I now regularly tell myself, "Ray, I am proud of you." And I mean it. It's uncomfortable at first. We're used to being hard on ourselves. Try it until it feels right.

  Pause and enjoy the little victories. To think you need to be serious all the time and move on to the next game is distorted thinking that leads to burnout. Savor the good moments. You aren't guaranteed another. Sports are cruel in that way.

- **Disqualifying the Positives Lenses:** This athlete hears "Good game" and shrugs it off with, "Only because the other team was terrible" or "Yeah, but so did everyone else." This athlete doesn't believe she deserves compliments and struggles to credit herself when it's due.

- **Removing the Disqualifying the Positive Lenses:** I asked an elite high school athlete when was the last time that he gave himself a compliment. "I don't think I ever have," he replied. Do you spin positive or neutral experiences into negatives? When was the last time you looked in the mirror, smiled, and told yourself, "I'm proud of you"? What might that do to your self-image and believing?

  If you keep discounting the positives in your life, you'll stay miserable even when bright moments shout your name. The bench player who finally sees playing time, only to complain the reason he's playing is because the starter got injured, is a typical example. This thinking keeps you from enjoying the moment and gaining positive momentum toward more playing time.

  Take time to write down some positive moments from each performance and visualize them. Then, compliment yourself and use your first name. We beat ourselves up using our first name. It's time to build that name up.

- **Mind-Reading Lenses:** This athlete's performance suffers based on what they *think* someone thinks of them.

- **Removing Mind-Reading Lenses:** It's impossible to know what someone thinks of you unless they genuinely tell you. Worrying about others' opinions will lead you down a dark rabbit hole of wasted focus and energy. It may be uncomfortable to ask your coach why you're not getting playing time, but the anguish of trying to read his or her mind will be far worse than any answer your coach provides.

  If you really must know something, go to the source and ask. Most people don't have it out for you. They're too focused on themselves. Get back to competing rather than fretting over what someone probably isn't even thinking about you. Better yet, stop caring what others think. That's where real freedom lives.

◆ **Fortune-Telling Lenses:** This athlete draws conclusions before the game even starts. She says, "We're probably going to lose" after watching the other team warm up. Or "We're not going to be that good this year" because last year's senior class graduated.

◆ **Removing the Fortune-Telling Lenses:** Catch yourself jumping to conclusions or setting expectations for how something might or must go. Negative expectations get confirmed the second you face adversity, and all you hear is, "I told you so." Quitting comes next. When you're playing better than expected, negative thinking asks, "When are things going to fall apart?" That's a lose-lose situation.

What if you set zero expectations except to go out and have fun competing to the best of your ability . . . one play at a time? That's what the 2004 Boston Red Sox did. With the odds and history stacked against them, the Red Sox came back from a 3-0 deficit in the American League Championship Series to beat the New York Yankees four straight games and then sweep the St. Louis Cardinals to win the World Series for the first time since 1918.

Had the Red Sox players told themselves, "The Yankees have been beating us for 100 years. No baseball team has ever come back from 3-0 to win a series. We might as well pack it up and call it a season," they would've never rewritten history with their improbable comeback.

Expectations and fortune-telling are traps. You have no clue what might happen on any given day. That's why you play the game. Play without expectations and let the final score tell the story. Don't give your free will to fate before the game or season even starts.

◆ **Emotional-Reasoning Lenses:** This athlete allows their feelings to become their truth. The stronger the feeling, the more real it must be.

- **Removing Emotional-Reasoning Lenses:** Emotions make sports fun. But they're dangerous. Decisions based on your emotional state often lead to regrets. Approach your sport with facts over feelings, no matter how strong your feelings. Also, learn to use your emotions as a gauge—not a guide. Your emotions will try to guide your actions. Don't allow them. Gauge how you feel, then allow your rational thinking to guide your next action. More on this later.

- **"Should Statement" Lenses:** High-achieving athletes who take it personally when they fail to meet unrealistic expectations.

- **Removing "Should Statement" Lenses:** I remember the day my counselor held her hand up to stop me from continuing one of my dramatic monologues about where I thought I should be in my life after the age of thirty. She kindly stated, "Ray, stop *shoulding* on yourself." Her words still make me laugh. But at the time, they made me pause and acknowledge how I was trying to steer my personal and professional life down some perfect path to success.

  When I finally stopped *shoulding* on myself (I still do occasionally), I freed myself up to:

  - Make mistakes
  - Have a bad day
  - Appreciate my accomplishments
  - Have patience with myself and situations I can't control
  - Make improvements rather than live in the shadows of my failures

  Yet is a powerful three-letter word that focuses on progress over perfection, so stop *shoulding* on yourself. Let go of where you think you should be and make the best of where you're at now.

- **Control-Fallacy Lenses:** These athletes either believe they need to control everything, or they believe they are helpless victims of fate and control nothing. Both options are lies.

- **Removing Control-Fallacy Lenses:** You have very little influence over what happens to you but complete control over how you think, feel, and respond. Austrian psychiatrist Viktor Frankl was imprisoned in a Nazi concentration camp where he had no control over his day-to-day life. Most people would regard his situation as being a helpless victim of fate. Yet, Frankl never thought that way because if he did, that way of thinking would get him killed or cause him to lose all hope.

  Despite living in hell on Earth, Frankl maintained hope that *today* he'd be rescued. Frankl had the least control anyone could have over their life, but the most control anyone could ever command over their mind. His example of controlling what was his to control speaks volumes to athletes who feel cheated by the system. You cannot control everything. But you can control the most important things—your mind and body. And, yes, Viktor Frankl got rescued on one of those *todays*.

- **Fairness Fallacy-Lenses:** This athlete believes sports should be fair.

- **Removing the Fairness-Fallacy Lenses:** Life and sports are unfair. Period. Minor League Baseball houses plenty of bonus babies making millions of dollars with a batting average of .180 who continue to start over the guy hitting .340 who signed for a plane ticket and $1,500 a month. It's politics and business, especially at the professional level.

  Athletes who insist sports should be fair will soon be out of a job and hanging out at the bar with bitterness, anger, and resentment. The reality is this: some athletes seem to be created for their sport and don't have to work nearly as hard. Unfair. Yet, the world owes you nothing, and the only thing you deserve is what you've earned. Once you accept that life and sports are unfair, you can focus on getting better rather than staying bitter.

- **Change-Fallacy Lenses:** In this athlete's mind, "if only" statements are frequent fliers. "If only I were getting consistent playing time I could ..." or "If only I didn't plant my foot and twist."

- **Removing the Change-Fallacy Lenses:** Wishing things were different than how they are creates resistance within you that'll only amplify your suffering and keep you stuck. If you're barely getting recruited right now, would you really make it to the Major Leagues *if only* you could get drafted? Would you really be stress-free *if only* you could secure a scholarship by your junior year in high school? Or would a new set of worries and expectations arise?

  The athletes who accept the reality around them are free to go after their goals. If you're not getting the playing time you want, make sure your performance in practice forces your coach to have a tough time deciding whether to play you or bench you for the next game. Make change happen. No one is going to change their policies for you. You'll be much happier when you control your attitude instead of trying to control your fate.

- **Heaven's Reward-Fallacy:** These athletes are most pitiable because they fully believe by doing all the right things, they'll be rewarded with all they ever wanted in their athletic career.

- **Removing Heaven's Reward-Fallacy Lenses:** Statistics show that less than one percent of athletes who set out to play professionally make it. As much as I hate luck, it does play a factor in who gets to the top. Plenty of the best athletes in the world never have their moment of glory. Is it hopeless for you?

  No. Understanding what little chance you have of playing professionally should light a fire in you to give everything you have while you have the opportunity. You're under no illusions that getting to the top and staying there will be easy.

  Those are some common cognitive distortions athletes encounter. If you've fallen victim to one or several of these lies, welcome to being human. Remain encouraged. We'll spend the remainder of this book deconstructing these and rebuilding your mindset from the neck up so you can focus on weathering the storms ahead.

  Next up, your identity.

Did any of those cognitive distortions resonate with you?

If so, post about it using #ThePillarBs
and tag @RenewedMindPerformance

1. Put on a pair of sunglasses to represent the lies
   you've been seeing your sport through

2. Then, while holding this book, name the cognitive
   distortion that's been telling you lies

3. Then, take off your sunglasses, and tell the world
   how you will no longer buy into the lie!

Section II

IDENTITY

6

YOUR WHO

"You have what most of us MLB players never did, true perspective. You didn't bow down & worship the game of baseball as if it were your God . . . You cared about the game but didn't let it define you the way we all did. Whether you were winning one of your three World Series titles or in the middle of a career-worst slump, you were the same Buster, focused, friendly, and always professional."

—Tweet from former MLB pitcher Barry Zito
about catcher Buster Posey's retirement

What's the difference between "I failed" and "I'm a failure"?

"I failed" defines what you did. "I'm a failure" defines who you are. If you're not careful, what you do and who you are begin to blur. It's fine when things are going well. But in sports, where things rarely go well for long, the emotional rollercoaster is a rough ride for those who identify primarily as athletes.

Falling short doesn't make you a failure. It confirms you're human.

Understand this: you are not your performance. You are not your sport. And while we're at it, you are not your thoughts, your emotions, or even your body. You are you, an ever-developing being who happens to have all sorts of thoughts, emotions, and bodily sensations. But *you* are none of them. Knowing this allows you to create distance and decide to what extent you want to identify with or be controlled by anything.

Getting caught up in your sport is easy if it's all you do, think about, and talk about. Your sport has given you status and popularity. It's almost impossible to escape it, even if you want to. It follows you from the field to the dinner table.

Your sport won't separate from you. You have to create separation from your sport. With so much failure wrapped up in sports, identifying as an athlete can ruin not only your believing, but your life and the lives around you.

SEPARATING SELVES

Chris, a professional baseball pitcher, was riding the performance roller coaster. After several bad outings, his wife knew to give him space, and recently, she'd been giving him plenty. When I asked him how he was doing, he shared that he got paid to get batters out, and when he didn't do his job, he felt like a failure and couldn't shake it.

He wasn't sleeping, feared being spotted in public, and was embarrassed to accept his paycheck. He started experiencing anxiety about going to the ballpark in anticipation of another poor performance. Fully identifying with his sport was costing him happiness in every category of his life.

He lit up when I asked him what it was like after pitching well. "If I play well, I deserve to go downtown to celebrate. But if I play bad, I don't deserve anything."

Unknowingly, Chris had built a mental prison around himself, and the gatekeeper was a cognitive distortion we discussed earlier called all-or-nothing thinking. His post-game life was dictated by how he performed because he couldn't separate who he was from what he did.

When your sport consumes your life, what you deserve or don't deserve gets based on an unfair reward system. Play well? You deserve a nice night. Play poorly? You deserve to suffer.

The temptation to identify with your performance only grows as you become more known for what you do than for who you are. Are you a victim of this mentality? As we deconstruct your relationship with your sport and reconstruct healthy boundaries, you'll be able to keep your confidence firmly intact and enjoy all aspects of life despite how you're playing.

My aim was to help Chris understand that he was not his performance. If he could detach from his sport, he could begin to put things back into proper perspective.

I showed him a clip from the movie *Fever Pitch*, starring Jimmy Fallon. Jimmy and his die-hard Boston Red Sox buddies are at a pub sulking over the playoff loss the Red Sox just took at the hands of their hated rival, the New York Yankees. One member of the group happens to look over at a table where three members of the Boston Red Sox were enjoying a post-game meal together and says, "Is that Jason Varitek? And Johnny Damon? And Trot?"

The others turn to see. "Yeah," they say in unison.

The guy who spotted them begins to unravel. "They're . . . *eating*?"

"So what?" Jimmy Fallon says.

"So *what*?" his friend repeats. "We're sitting here dining on our guts over the Red Sox, and there's three members *of* the Red Sox eating . . . with gusto!"

One of the guys turns back to the bar stone-faced. "Ironic," he declares.

"Ironic?" says another one. "Ted Williams would roll over in his freezer if he saw this."

Jimmy Fallon chimes in, "Why shouldn't they eat? They played hard. They did their best. What more could you want?"

This scene is quite sobering. The Red Sox players, who had more to lose than anyone, were able to separate their work lives from their personal lives. Were they happy to be down 3-0 in a series where no team had ever come back in 2004? Probably not. But they also weren't dragging their job into every other part of their lives. In this situation, they were the winners. They knew baseball was part of their life, not all of it. Like Jimmy Fallon said, they played hard and did their best. Can anyone do more than that? Can you?

I asked Chris what he thought of the clip. Although he enjoyed it and understood the point, he still had a tough time with the idea of not beating himself up over poor performances. Habits die hard. When you choose to step back and view your performance for what it truly is, one uniquely isolated incident in time and not a reflection of who you are as a person, it'll keep you from magnifying the moment and eating yourself alive.

When you keep in mind that you are not your performance, you're capable of loving yourself, giving and receiving love, and feeling accepted, no matter how you perform. Your self-worth doesn't have to be based on a reward system of wins and losses.

Does your dog care whether you won or lost? He loves you because you're you. Treat yourself similarly. Then, life will be sweet despite what's happening on the field. You'll also be able to genuinely root for others when they're playing well—even if you're not.

FREEDOM FROM FAILURE

Page Odle, head agent and owner of PSI Sports Performance, told me a story about his first breakout client, long-time Pittsburg Pirate short-stop Jack Wilson. When Jack came up as a rookie, Page watched most of Jack's at-bats on TV or in person.

Jack ended up striking out seventy times out of 425 at-bats in 2001. After a while, Page asked Jack why he didn't seem to care when he struck out. He told Page, "I do care. But if I get upset every time I strike out, my career would've been over a long time ago. I hope I strike out 10,000 more times. If I do, that means I get to play this game for a really long time."

I share this story with athletes who identify too closely with their failures. While with the Pirates for nine years, Jack never experienced a winning season. That's a lot of losing. His lifetime on-base percentage was .306. That means about 70 percent of the time, he failed at his job on offense.

An abundance of losing and failure will eat at anyone. Yet, Jack's ability to separate himself from his struggles on offense allowed him to excel as one of the best defensive shortstops in the MLB for twelve seasons. Even more importantly, his ability to leave his cleats at the field rather than bring the mud home permitted him to savor life outside of baseball with his family and friends.

How might you benefit from truly separating yourself from your sport once the game is over? How might it impact your confidence and self-worth?

Benefits of separating your personal from performance life:

+ Overall happiness
+ Healthy self-worth
+ Proper sport/life perspective
+ Quicker performance rebounds
+ Greater peace of mind (not worried about others' opinions)

Detriments of mixing personal and performance life:

+ Depression
+ Anxiety
+ Self-Critical
+ Unhealthy sport/life balance
+ Delayed rebound during slumps or poor play
+ Wasted energy focused on others' opinions

If you're no longer your performance, then who are you? You are a combination of your likes, dislikes, hobbies, interests, and intellect, to name a few qualities. Your identity is yours to discover.

FREEDOM IN THE IDENTITY SHIFT

Answering who you are, if you're not your performance, starts with asking: "What's it like when I fully identify with my sport?"

You can't appreciate the freedom of separating from your sport until you grasp how shackling it is to identify with it solely. Write down your answer to that question before reading the following quotes compiled from clients who've found themselves at times (or often) fully identifying with their sport:

1. "It consumes my entire life. I can't enjoy anything else if I'm playing bad. Nothing else matters besides my sport. Even if we're playing at a cool tournament location, I'll lock myself in my hotel room and close the blinds if I'm playing bad."

2. "If I have a bad tournament, it's hard to forget. Plays I messed up years ago still run through my head every day."

3. "I'm competitive at everything. It's really stressful, actually. School too. But my sport comes first, more than anything. My parents try to tell me there's more to life and more to me than my sport. I just find that hard to believe, I guess."

4. "I have high expectations. I let things go pretty quickly the next day. But if I have a bad game, it's going to beat me up the rest of that day for sure."

5. "I mean, my sport is everything to me. It's the only thing I love right now. Every part of my life: how I eat, how often I work out, how I plan my day is all built around my sport."

6. "Vacation? That scares me. If I'm not working out every day, I feel lost, like I'm losing progress and will have to start all over, even if it's just a few days away from the gym. It even sounds crazy when I say it out loud. But that's just the way it is. I wouldn't be able to relax or enjoy myself on vacation because I'll be thinking about everyone getting better than me."

These are typical thought patterns from athletes who heavily identify with their sport. Do any of these ring a bell with you? It's okay if they do.

I then asked these athletes to consider what life and sport would be like if their sport became what they did instead of who they are. The main response from everyone? Smiles of hope mixed with hopelessness. Each said about the same thing: "Everything would be much more enjoyable."

I pressed further by having each of them write down how life and sport might be different if they chose to see sport as what they do instead of who they are. I gave them this prompt: "If my sport becomes what I do rather than who I am . . ." Their replies:

1. "I'd be able to enjoy life no matter how I'm performing. I think I would care less. Not in effort, but like, be less attached to every outcome and every play. I'd be able to have fun on the court more and not care as much about what other people think of me. I'd probably play better. I'd explore cool towns with teammates when we're not playing. I could leave my performance on the court and go back to my hotel and be okay with myself. I'd probably like myself more."

2. "I could learn from my performances rather than beat myself up about them. I could do my best to let them go. I may never forget them, but I could try not to repeat those mistakes. When those memories come to me, I can say, 'That's what I did. It's not who I am.'"

3. "I can still be competitive, but it doesn't have to stress me out. I can remember it's just a game. It's not my whole world. I think

75

being competitive is important, but it doesn't have to rule my life. I can relax a bit more I guess, especially if I know something doesn't need to stress me out. I think it would be good to find other activities to enjoy besides my sport—something else for balance. I'm realizing how much my sport consumes my life. It's kind of scary."

4. "Even as I'm talking, I'm realizing some of my high expectations are impossible expectations. If they're unreachable, I can't ever be satisfied or happy. I think if I lower my expectations or at least make them attainable, I will be happier and nicer to myself. I guess right now I'm not very nice to myself. It's scary to think about lowering my expectations, though."

5. "If my sport becomes what I do rather than who I am, I don't know. That's hard. Would people still like me? Everything, well, a lot of things, would be different. But I can see how it might be good to care about other things going on in life. Like a hobby or something. I guess I wouldn't work out as much."

6. "I'd probably be able to relax on vacation. Like, actually be there on vacation rather than dwelling on my sport and what I'm missing. I would probably sleep in. [Smiling] I guess that's what vacation is for. I'd be able to give my body and mind a rest. Which could be good. One time I didn't work out for like a week and then did a max bench press and lifted more than I ever have. So, maybe rest isn't such a bad thing."

What would your life and sports career be like if you chose to allow your sport to be what you do rather than who you are? Where would you experience more freedom? What might happen to your self-worth? Take a moment and answer the following: "If my sport becomes what I do rather than who I am . . ."

After answering, your perspective might shift from "I'm a failure" to "I failed today, but I'm no failure." You want to move from, "How could

I be this terrible? I don't deserve to go out with friends" to "That was a tough loss, but I'm no loser. Losses will happen. But I can still hang with friends to get my mind off the game."

What freedom in the shift!

You are much more than your sport. Your self-worth no longer needs to be tangled up with your performance. You are worthy of love despite how you play because every person is worthy of love. You are worthy of acceptance whether you win or lose because your acceptance is not based on the outcome of some game. Unconditional love must first start with yourself. You can't depend on anyone else to extend it to you. Become your greatest support system.

The idea that you are more than your sport can be uncomfortable to consider. There is a sense of protection and popularity in hiding behind your sport—at least when things are going well. But it'll be even more uncomfortable when your athletic career is over and you're left with an identity crisis. Develop your identity outside of sport *now* with your friends, your interests, your hobbies, or your future career path, so you have something to fall back on during and after your career.

When you have hobbies that absorb you, it's a great way to decompress from competition and a reminder that you're good at other things besides sports. Friends and family who enjoy talking about topics beyond sports can be a welcome distraction. When you volunteer or give back to your community, it helps put your athletic career in proper perspective. These, and other ways of expressing who you are, help remind you that you're more than your sport.

No matter how good you are, your sport will one day go on without you. Then, who will you be? Kobe Bryant didn't wait until his career with the Lakers was over to start thinking about what was next. He opened the Mamba Sports Academy facilities in Thousand Oaks and Redondo Beach for current and aspiring athletes and wrote children's fantasy books. LeBron James has emerged as one of Hollywood's hottest producers, even while still in the NBA. Kobe found a deeper purpose beyond basketball. LeBron continues to use his platform to improve the next generation of youth.

You have permission to pursue interests and dreams beyond athletics. If you're like most athletes, your full focus right now is on making it to the elite level of your sport. And that's good. But along the way, you'll miss out on a lot that life has to offer if you only have tunnel vision for professional sports.

Are you putting all your self-worth in the athlete basket? Or are you a person who has other areas of interest but happens to compete athletically at a high level? Can you work to make your sport just one of many aspects that make you unique?

KNOWING WHO YOU ARE NOT

With the first pick in the 1999 MLB draft, the Tampa Bay Devil Rays selected high school phenom Josh Hamilton out of Raleigh, North Carolina. After signing for about $4 million, Josh promptly won Minor League Player of the Year in 2000 and was on the fast track in spring training of 2001 to make the Major League roster and rescue the drowning Devil Rays. So, how is it then that Hamilton didn't make his Major League debut until April 2, 2007—with the Reds?

Prior to the 2001 season, Josh was in a serious car accident that left him in constant pain. Around the same time, the Devil Rays organization felt it would be best for Josh's maturation if his parents, who had quit their jobs to follow his minor league career, returned home and left Josh to grow up on his own.

All at once, a teenage Josh Hamilton, with millions of dollars and no parental support during his first injury-plagued season, was left to figure out who he was without baseball.

To escape the physical pain and the mental pressure from the Devil Rays urging him to play through injuries, Josh began spending most of his time away from the field at tattoo parlors to numb out with ink.

When tattoos weren't enough, he turned to drinking and drugs. How could a young star with nothing but greatness attached to his name find himself falling so far?

There were two major motivators: a desire for acceptance and a need to escape the pain.

Everyone needs acceptance, even if it's with the wrong crowd. And no one enjoys pain, even if it takes numbing out the wrong way.

In his book, *Beyond Belief*, Hamilton shared that the guys at the tattoo parlor didn't care that he was a superstar baseball player. They didn't even like baseball. They cared that he paid for his tattoos and was a cool guy.

While unable to play consistently due to the pain, Josh's baseball career continued to take a backseat to unhealthy lifestyle choices. Between 2001 and 2006, Hamilton was repeatedly suspended from minor league baseball for positive drug tests. In 2006, the Devil Rays finally cut ties with him. He signed with the Chicago Cubs and was immediately traded to the Cincinnati Reds.

After making his Major League debut in April 2007 with the Reds as an outfielder, Hamilton was traded to the Texas Rangers, where between 2008 and 2012, he showed the world a glimpse of what could've been. In a stunted career, Hamilton accumulated a career batting average of .290 with 200 career home runs, two World Series appearances, five All-Star games, and was the 2010 American League MVP.

Hamilton's genetic makeup, work ethic, and skillset were a gift to baseball, and his career was primed to be one for the ages. Had a few life events and personal choices gone differently, who knows what his career numbers would've been and what personal pain he could've skipped. But again, can we really blame him? If you were in similar circumstances, are you sure you wouldn't have fallen into the same dark place?

Will you become a *what could've been*? Or will you make time to establish who you truly are by drawing a line in the sand between what you will and won't stand for? The pressures and pleasures of life will come at you quick. They came at Josh and stole his best playing years.

If you don't know who you are, you will likely become someone you never intended to be. Had Josh been able to separate his identity from his sport, it would've been easier to handle the setbacks with a much healthier approach. That would have served his career rather than stolen it.

Drawing a line in the sand starts with establishing your core values. Your core values will be the guardrails that keep you on the path toward your dreams and help you navigate life's tough moments and decisions.

We've spent a good deal of time on your *who* because without it, your *why* doesn't matter. Remind yourself daily who you really are so you can focus on what's next—your *why*.

7

YOUR WHY

In the book *Start with Why*, author Simon Sinek says your *why* is your purpose, cause, or belief behind what you do. Your *why* is what springs you out of bed in the morning. It's your innermost calling.

Apple Computer's *why* in the late 1970s was and remains to this day: challenge the status quo. They carry out their *why* through their *what*, which is building computers, smartphones, and electronic devices for the masses.

Your sport is your *what*. That's the easy part. But have you considered your *why*? What calling drives you to devote so much time, effort, and energy to pursuing your sport?

THE IMPORTANCE OF A COMPELLING WHY

In my last chapter, I introduced you to Josh Hamilton, the No. 1 baseball draft pick in 1999. While his trajectory had him landing in the big leagues by 2001, he didn't appear in a Major League game until 2007 due to injuries, drugs, and alcohol issues. How did Hamilton go from six years of darkness to one of the brightest stars in baseball from 2008 through 2012?

He found a worthy *why*.

When Josh decided he'd hit rock bottom, he reached out to the last person still holding out hope for him—his grandma. She not only nursed him back to life physically, but she also fed him spiritually. She gave him a Bible, which he read daily. He started attending church and asked God to heal his mind and body from all the self-inflicted damage he'd caused. Even he knew he shouldn't be alive.

Hamilton prayed. God answered.

Once Major League Baseball reinstated Josh from his suspension, he had a new *why* fueling him. His life was no longer about money, notoriety, lifestyle, or the Hall of Fame. He was about one thing: sharing the good news of Jesus Christ and how the love of God can rescue anyone—even him. That was Hamilton's *why*. Baseball was his *what*.

Josh let his *why* be known, whether he was talking one-on-one with a fan or putting on a show during the 2008 Home Run Derby at Yankee Stadium. Anyone who knew anything about him knew what he stood for and why he played the game. Every workout, batting practice, and fielding session to improve his skills were fueled by his desire to share his faith.

Your *why* will be unique to you. It's not my job to tell you if your *why* is worthy enough. Only you can answer that. Just make sure that *why* burns in your chest every day to the point you jump out of bed with a laser-like focus ready to take massive action.

Once you establish a compelling *why*, nothing gets easier, however. Life actually gets harder. The second you set your *why*, like *really* set your *why*, it'll be challenged immediately. *Is that really why you play?*

Josh Hamilton's *why* was put to the test every day of his career. His old habits didn't just go away. Temptations to seek pleasure or relieve pressure through drugs and alcohol came at him constantly. They were immediate, enticing, and impulsive urges from within to discredit him as a Christian athlete.

Hamilton had to keep his *why*—his purpose, his calling—front and center and more desirable than any pressure or pleasure. Each time he overcame a temptation, it made him stronger and more convinced of his *why* and more eager to share his faith.

Similarly, once Apple set their *why* of challenging the status quo, the tech company knew it could never take shortcuts or launch a product that wasn't pushing the envelope. Apple wasn't the first company to come up with the MP3 player. But when they introduced the iPod that put "one thousand songs in your pocket" and paired it with iTunes, it literally changed how people bought and listened to music. Their *why* continues to push them beyond the ordinary to become revolutionary.

What's your *why*?

If you're willing to establish a concrete *why* now, you won't need to soul search later. Apple knew their *why* early on, which helped them weather the ups and downs every company faces. Josh Hamilton hit rock bottom before discovering his *why*. But once he found his, it compelled him to resurrect his baseball career and showcase his greatness.

Their *why*'s weren't focused on reaching the top. They became elite in their respective industries as a byproduct of sticking to their *why*. Without their *why*, neither Apple nor Josh Hamilton would've likely made it or stayed there for long. Their *why*'s were focused more on impacting others than on how it would benefit themselves.

Crucial to a worthy *why* is how your *what* will impact others, as in, what's it all for anyways?

Had Apple not held firmly to their *why*, we wouldn't have the high-quality, easy-to-use devices we didn't know we needed. Apple's *why* drives them to design products that allow their users to further their careers, connect with others easily, and capture life's precious moments. Today, millions of people are benefiting from Apple's *why*.

Had Josh Hamilton budged on his *why* during his comeback, countless individuals wouldn't have witnessed his triumphant comeback or heard him share his testimony. Josh's *why* inspired thousands of down-and-out individuals to find hope. Thousands, if not millions, benefited from one person with a worthy *why*, sharing his message that carried both a temporary and eternal impact.

For what cause or purpose are you willing to sacrifice mediocrity for disciplined action so you can positively impact others? How will others be better off because you played the game? Apple is one company. Josh Hamilton was one athlete. But their impacts have each been astronomical. You are one person.

How will your *why* influence others?

ACCOUNTABILITY TO YOUR WHY

I knew a married couple who had "Remember Why" taped to the fridge. I'll call them Cali and Jeff Lackey. Each of them had grown up in families where money was a limiting factor. As adults, Cali and Jeff were determined to not overspend now for financial freedom later. Financial freedom was their *why*. "Remember Why" was their daily reminder that each money decision would either help or hurt them reach financial freedom. They learned to be content living on less in the short term, so they could live and give like no one else in the long term.

What tangible proof showed they were living their *why*? Each month, the Lackeys agreed to a $200 a month discretionary spending allowance for each of them. Beyond $200, they needed each other's permission to spend, and it had to be for necessities like groceries. This caused them to consider each purchase carefully rather than spend mindlessly. Anytime Cali or Jeff wanted to complain or go over budget, the other spouse just pointed to the fridge as accountability to their *why*. Accountability to financial freedom.

Keeping each other in check helped the Lackeys weather any immediate pressure or pleasure trying to persuade them out of their long-term *why*. Together, they were stubborn about their *why*, which all started with wanting a better life than the one they were brought up in.

What will be your daily accountability to keep your *why* the apple of your eye?

WHAT'S REALLY FUELING YOUR WHY?

When I ask clients about their *why*, most immediately respond, "It's what I've always wanted." But when I ask them why they feel that way, the pauses grow longer. Most athletes don't know why they *really* want to play professionally. Do you? If your current *why* is money or fame, there are plenty of professional athletes who "have it all" but still feel empty. If you don't know your true *why*, welcome to the crowd. Keep asking why until you reach your bedrock *why*.

When I met with Kelly, a high school volleyball client, and inquired about her *why*, she replied, "I guess I love a really nice dig or pass that perfectly sets up a teammate for a kill." A nice *why*. As she talked it out, she realized those were tangible pieces of evidence of her true *why*: "I love doing whatever I can to build confidence in others."

That's bedrock.

For Kelly, the mindset wasn't, "I play my sport so I can earn a scholarship," as much as it was, "I love to set others up for success and celebrate with them. A scholarship in volleyball will help me do that."

Same *what*. Different *why*. And it adds up to a better work ethic. The byproduct of her *why*—earning a scholarship—would also further her education so she could one day make a career out of helping others build their confidence. Same *why*. Different *what*. Knowing your *why* can help you determine where you will thrive best.

Another client, Jesse, had verbally committed to a Division 1 powerhouse baseball school on the West Coast. When he received news he'd been accepted into the Air Force Academy, however, he knew where he belonged.

When Jesse had to explain to everyone why he was de-committing from a baseball powerhouse to play for the Air Force Academy, he confidently shared how the Air Force Academy was more aligned with the man he wanted to become and how he wanted to impact his country. From a sports standpoint, the Air Force Academy was less shiny to outsiders but fully aligned with Jesse's *why*.

The importance of Jesse knowing his *why before* college was life-changing. I've seen too many athletes pick a college for its fame over its fit. Rarely does it work out for either side that way. Many athletes who choose a school not based on their *why* either burn out due to not meshing with the coaching staff or never get an opportunity to play.

A strong *why* gives you the clarity and wisdom to make the best choices for you based on the information available. A strong *why* can also be the difference in withstanding or falling to the pressures and pleasures trying to derail you on and off the field.

ENEMIES OF YOUR WHY

Former NFL player Asante Cleveland told me there were over thirty players in his football recruiting class at the University of Miami. By the season opener, only fourteen recruits remained. What happened? These players were only one step away from playing for a major college football program, yet the immediate pressures and pleasures available nonstop in Miami were too strong for their *why*.

What pleasures and pressures will threaten your *why*? No matter how straight-edged you are right now, no matter if you've never done drugs or drank alcohol or fooled around sexually, whatever your weakness is, the world will expose you if your *why* isn't bold enough.

If you think you're invincible, consider Josh Hamilton one more time. The success of being the No. 1 draft pick, having millions of dollars in the bank, and being a phone call away from the Big Leagues at twenty years old was no match for the pressures and pleasures awaiting him after a serious car crash threatened his career.

Drugs, alcohol, and tattoos—words never before associated with Josh Hamilton's name—became his escape. They instantly eased the pressure the Tampa Bay Devil Rays put on him as their top prospect and future savior. Drugs and alcohol provided pleasure and momentarily erased the pain of knowing how close he was to greatness. Short-term gratification cost him long-term satisfaction.

Half of Asante Cleveland's recruiting class at Miami either couldn't make grades or broke team policy and had their dreams cut down before they began. They succumbed to the pressures and pleasures of the world. You will too unless you have a worthy *why*. Pressures and pleasures are enemies of your *why*.

Pressures include the temptation to use performance-enhancing drugs to keep up or level up. Or the need to appear tough by owning guns or acting violent. Pleasures include partying, drugs, alcohol, and sexual promiscuity. These pressures and pleasures will all be available in abundance. You won't have to look for them. They'll find you.

Success, which is a powerful pleasure, is one of the most subtle enemies of your *why*. If Apple's *why* wasn't to challenge the status quo, they would've gotten complacent after surpassing Microsoft. Had Josh Hamilton not established that his career was no longer about himself but about his personal relationship with Jesus Christ, he would've stopped sharing his testimony after becoming a superstar.

SUBTLE SURPRISES IN THE SACRIFICE

Let me be clear. To get where few ever go, you need to be willing to sacrifice what others won't let go. This is a hard concept in our world of FOMO (fear of missing out). Today's athletes feel entitled to the shine without the grind. The bright lights without the dark fights.

The grind isn't glamorous. It's rarely fun. That's why it's called the grind. What did the grind look like for Cali and Jeff on that $200-a-month budget? It meant taking lunches to work. Making coffee at home instead of picking up Philz Coffee or Starbucks. Saying no to opportunities to go on out-of-town trips with friends. This couple was willing to do what most others wouldn't so they could live later like most others couldn't.

The Lackeys soon realized there were hidden benefits behind their sacrifices. Making their lunch and drinking their own coffee saved time, money, and mental energy in decision-making. Saying no to opportunities they couldn't strongly say yes to became easier.

When Cali and Jeff stopped stretching themselves beyond their means, their stress levels dropped, and they grew to treasure simplicity in the little things. How many people spend money they don't have, complain of never having enough time, and burn themselves out trying to please everyone? These are people who lack a convincing *why*. What surprises await you when you are willing to sacrifice for your *why*?

WHAT IS YOUR WHY WILLING TO SACRIFICE?

If I was to spend a day with you, how would I see you living out your *why*? If you are only willing to sacrifice the same as everyone else, you can't expect to gain anything different than them.

What does the short-term sacrifice look like for you? Skipping parties to maximize your sleep, safety, and health? Limiting social media to make quality time for homework or in-person meetups? Cutting out unhealthy foods that may taste good on the lips but go straight to your hips?

Kelly's *why* was to do whatever she could to build her teammates' confidence. That meant she had to sacrifice the glory her teammates received for smashing volleyballs over the net. But without her working hard to set them up, they wouldn't have a chance to do their part so well. That's where Kelly found internal satisfaction. Only people who know the intricacies of volleyball could appreciate her skill set. Compliments meant more to her because they were coming from people who knew the game.

The right sacrifices have your best interests in mind. When you're willing to sacrifice for the right *why*, you'll never regret saying goodbye.

WHAT'S YOUR WHY WILLING TO DO?

Your *why* must not only sacrifice more but be willing to do more. Boston Red Sox Hall of Famer Ted Williams famously walked into empty baseball stadiums and shouted, "I'm the greatest hitter in the world!"

Baseball was his *what*. Having people walk down the street and say, "There goes the greatest hitter who ever lived," was his *why*. What was he willing to do to make that a reality?

Hitting became Ted Williams' obsession. There wasn't a detail too small for him. He hit until his hands bled. Then he developed calluses so he could hit more. He traveled with a scale to weigh his bats before games to ensure they were to his specification. Hitting was a science to Ted, so much so that he wrote a book, *The Science of Hitting*. He was willing to do what it took to become the best.

What is your *why* willing to do?

Put in extra gym time or get private lessons? Work with a mental performance coach? Seek out top technological resources to unearth the difference between good and great? Consistently eat healthy and get to bed early?

Whatever it takes, take it on. Your time in sports is short. Make the most of your minutes by doing what others aren't willing to do. It's better to make the effort now than dwell on your career the rest of your life wishing you could go back. Maybe you don't care to be like Ted Williams and have people refer to you as the *best who ever lived*, but make sure your *why* is so strong that you're more than willing to do what it takes to fulfill it.

YOUR WHY DOESN'T GUARANTEE ANYTHING

A great *why* doesn't mean anything unless you take consistent action aligned with it. Talent will only get you so far. Talent combined with a compelling *why* will get you as far as you're capable of going. There's a rude awakening for those who choose not to establish a personal *why*. There's only so much room at the top for even the best. But absolutely no room for those with a weak *why*.

Is your *why* transferable? Apple used to be called Apple Computers at one time. When they began making other products, they simply became Apple. Same *why*, expanded *what*. Someday, your sports career will end. Will your *why* die with your athletic career, or will a new *what* sign your *why* like a free agent?

Kelly's *why* for setting others up for success was transferable from the volleyball court to a future career. With a compelling *why*, your transition out of sport someday will be smoother as you can continue pursuing your *why* with a new *what*. If not, emptiness and confusion await you.

Either way, it's not an easy road. Setbacks will frustrate you, and pressures and pleasures will ambush you. But when you truly connect with your *why* and remind yourself daily why you play your sport, every decision simply becomes, "Does what I'm about to do align with my *why*?" There will be only one right answer.

Now that you know *who* you are and *why* you play, you'll need to determine *how* you'll get where you're going.

8

YOUR HOW

James Shields earned the nickname "Big Game James" for his gutsy performances and ability to pitch deep into baseball games. From 2007 to 2015, he was one of the top pitchers in baseball, including an All-Star nod in 2011.

I was affiliated with his sports agency when I was invited to watch him pitch for the Tampa Bay Rays versus the Anaheim Angels during the 2008 season. After the Friday night game at Angel Stadium, a slew of his family and friends were at the team hotel catching up with him when several of his buddies started badgering him to go out for a round of drinks.

Without hesitation, he hit the elevator button and said, "I'm pitching tomorrow. I gotta get some rest, but after the game, we'll have some fun." He and his wife disappeared into the elevator, and that was that.

Shields was completely fine saying no to his closest friends who rarely got to see him. Why? Because he prioritized pitching over having a good time. James' pre-game preparation wasn't a core value that he happened to develop once he reached the Major Leagues. That's likely what got him there in the first place.

Every day you'll have to decide what's most important to you. Sometimes your values will clash, like spending time with loved ones or doing your pre-game preparation. Shields knew a good night's sleep would help him pitch to the best of his ability the following day. Staying out with friends until the wee hours wouldn't.

Most athletes know the *how* of what it takes to get to the top, but few are willing to consistently do what's necessary to get there. Shields lived his *how*. He also knew his decisions impacted more than just himself. The Rays went on to play in the World Series that year, perhaps in part to guys like James Shields who valued their *how*.

Life in sports is full of detours ready and willing to veer your *what* and *why* off the professional path. Your *how* will be the guardrails to help you make sound decisions and keep you on course. After talent, your success or failure largely depends on the core values you establish and refuse to budge on.

Here's my question: What do you really care about?

WHAT YOU CARE ABOUT IS WHAT YOU EMPHASIZE

If you ever want to know what someone values, just watch what they do and listen to what they say. A person's actions, words, and habits show you what they deem important. If you're anxious to log on for another round of Call of Duty right before and after games, that's what you value.

Ask yourself where you devote your time and energy. Your answers point to what you value. If you're unhappy with how you're allocating your time and energy, change where you devote those precious resources.

FIND PLEASURE IN WHAT YOU MEASURE

Check out this quote:

"I know that just as I am refining my pitching, I am refining the pleasure I get from it. A victory used to give me pleasure, then a well-pitched inning, and now I get satisfaction from just

one or two pitches a game. I get in a situation where I have
to apply all I know, mentally, physically, on just one pitch."

—Tom Seaver, Hall of Fame Pitcher,
from Harvey Dorfman's *The Mental ABC'S of Pitching*

As your perspective matures, so should what you value. As Seaver matured, he simplified what was important to him. Rather than measuring success and failure on wins and losses, which were largely outside his control, he began to find great pleasure in being totally enthralled in each pitch he threw. "Terrific Tom," as he was called, changed what gave him pleasure. When he began to emphasize the importance of each pitch, he privately experienced little wins in seeing the ball do exactly what he wanted it to do. These private wins fueled him to become one of the greatest pitchers of his generation.

How do you measure your performance? Having the right metrics allows you to experience pleasure even when you lose. When you measure the wrong metrics, you can experience heartache even when you win.

In a Netflix documentary called *The Playbook*, Patrick Mouratoglou, Serena Williams' former tennis coach, was interviewed alongside one of his rising tennis stars at the time, Irena Pavlovic. The reporter asked Irena how she felt about being ranked No. 1 in France for her age bracket in junior tennis.

With a dissatisfied shrug, Irena said, "It's okay."

"Just okay?"

"Well . . . I want to be No. 1 in the world."

Throughout this book, you've been asked to believe in yourself as the best in the world. It's a mindset. But being consumed with becoming No. 1 in the world to the dissatisfaction of anything less is having a mind set on disappointment. Pavlovic was blind to how good she was due to her dissatisfaction. Throughout the documentary, she never exudes joy, often beats herself up mentally and physically, and admits she tanked matches if losing to an inferior opponent. That way, if she gave up, she could tell herself she didn't lose.

Tom Seaver was inducted into the baseball Hall of Fame at least partly due to how he defined success and the pleasure he got from little personal victories. The highest world ranking Pavlovic ever earned in tennis was No. 136 (which is still incredible). Who knows how high she would've climbed had she learned to treasure private wins rather than suffer public blowups? From the perspective of the documentary, her only measuring stick of success was achieving No. 1 in the world. Anything less was failure. She found no pleasure in what she measured.

What you value and how you measure it should be geared toward boosting your believing rather than tearing it down. What Tom Seaver measured made him better. What Irena Pavlovic measured made her worse. Does what you measure boost your confidence or burst it? Is what you're measuring an accurate indicator of how you perform?

A Division 1 softball client told me that as a freshman, she measured her success by whether her name was featured in the game recap on the team website. When her teammate, an established senior, put up similar numbers and received more press, my client viewed her performance as a failure. Is whether your name makes the postgame article a good measuring tool of success? No.

We measure what we value. Make sure what you measure is in your control and can lead to pleasure. Getting your name in the paper is outside your control because you're not the one writing the article. So why measure yourself by it? Being No. 1 in the world is largely outside your control because you can't control your competition. So why base your entire self-worth on it? Get to the point where your private progress reports are just as satisfying as your public wins.

YOUR VALUES DETERMINE YOUR DILEMMAS

You're going to deal with dilemmas, drama, and problems throughout your athletic career. That's life. Your values will help determine whether you have good problems or bad ones. Good problems based on good values might be whether to go to the gym or get in extra work after practice. Whether to have the BBQ chicken salad or a steak sandwich for dinner.

Bad dilemmas based on poor values include which bar to go to tonight. Whether to drink or smoke, or both. Which attractive person to take home. Which adult sites to browse. Whether to use performance-enhancing drugs or not.

When you establish good values, those bad dilemmas and drama become easy noes. Yet, one bad decision based on poor values can lead to more difficult problems to navigate. Las Vegas wide receiver, Henry Ruggs, discovered this the hard way.

After a Raiders home game on November 1, 2021, Ruggs decided to party on the Vegas Strip late into the night. At four in the morning, with a blood alcohol level of .16 (twice the legal limit), Ruggs, along with his girlfriend, zipped home at speeds above 150 mph through residential neighborhoods. Only a mile from his house, Ruggs slammed his Corvette into the back of a small SUV at over 120 mph, setting the SUV ablaze. The driver in the SUV and her dog were killed. Ruggs and his girlfriend were badly injured. The Raiders released him the next day. A woman died needlessly, and his NFL career was over.

Values guide your decisions. Your decisions determine your dilemmas.

There's no doubt Henry Ruggs valued his football career. But in the moment, he valued a good time over his football career. His choice to party set up a domino effect of poor decisions that followed. There's nothing wrong with having fun after a game. But why not set boundaries and guidelines to ensure a good time and a safe return home for everyone?

Ruggs obviously wasn't hurting for cash. Why not spend a hundred dollars on a driving service? Instead, he chose to drive home drunk. Why not drive the speed limit? Instead, he sipped a mixed cocktail called ego and a fast car. His choices, based on what *he* valued at the time, resulted in the end of another young person's life and his football career before either of them had a chance to gain real yardage in this world.

Remember, your values inform your decisions. Your decisions

determine your dilemmas. Choose to establish good values that lead to good problems instead of living the rest of your life wishing you had.

WHAT YOU VALUE DETERMINES YOUR ATTITUDE

In baseball, base running is shrugged off by most of the team. Yet, if your legs are your strength, you might get excited about base running drills because that's where you excel.

In basketball, you might dread repetitively running plays. Yet, if you're a point guard who values precision, your attitude toward running plays might be different from the teammate who's going through the motions until shooting practice.

What are the areas of your sport you dread, and what do you anticipate? What you dread reveals areas you value less. Can you find it in you to bring enthusiasm to each area of your sport? Whether it's bunting, ladder drills, running routes, or wind sprints, they're all valuable to helping you become the best version of yourself.

But if you shirk the work, you'll get exposed when it matters most. You don't have to love every aspect of practice, but you at least have to respect it enough to give it everything you have each day.

THREE TYPES OF ATHLETE VALUES

In *Mental Toughness*, authors Karl and John Kuehl and Casey Tefertiller describe three sets of values important to the athlete: personal values, performance values, and team values.

- **Personal Values:** Former NFL and University of Miami football player Asante Cleveland, whom we discussed earlier, shared with me about his morning routine: "I never know how a day is going to go. But I always know how it's going to start. *That* I can control," he said. Asante is willing to rise early to journal, stretch, and breathe.

The impact those three activities have on his day allows him to show up at his best for himself and others.

For me, I value integrity and living to the best of my ability by the core value: *Do the harder thing.* That means no matter what I'm doing, I take the path of most resistance. When my dog goes to the bathroom on someone's lawn and no one is watching, I pick up after him anyways. Why? I do the harder thing. When I'm tempted to throw my dish in the sink instead of washing it, I'm compelled to walk back and not only wash my dish but any other dirty dishes that someone else left. Why? Because it's the harder thing.

There are incredible benefits to doing the harder thing. I'll share two and leave the others for you to discover. Number one: your mind begins to tell you the right thing to do. Most minds look for the easy way out. But by consistently doing the harder thing, you train your brain to demand the harder course of action.

The second benefit: the harder thing becomes your normal thing. Your norm becomes everyone else's harder thing. Advantage you. These are just a few examples of personal values. What personal values will you establish to help you get where you want to go?

♦ **Performance Values:** If I asked your coaches about you, would they tell me you're early to practice, take the young players under your wing, are detail-oriented, and know when to focus and when to have fun? Or would they tell me something else?

If I asked you to write up a practice plan, your design would show me what you value. If you designed an hour-long lacrosse practice and broke it into forty minutes devoted to shooting on goal, fifteen minutes of defensive drills, and five minutes of passing skills, you'd let me know quickly what you see as most important.

James Shields' pre-game preparation was so important to him that it started the night before. The best in the world have their pre-game routines down to the minute because they know preparation leads to confidence and comfort. What they can control, they control. They don't measure whether their pre-game routine is successful based on their stat sheet. They measure it by whether it prepared them to battle to the best of their abilities. That's what's in their control.

A Division 1 baseball client casually told me, "Well, practice starts at 3:30, so I get there by 2:30." It wasn't mandatory for him to be there an hour early, but he valued how his preparation routines allowed him to compete in practice with the same intensity as a game. It's no wonder he got drafted in 2022.

Do you show up on time, hoping everything falls into place? Are you more interested in squeezing in twenty minutes of video games than establishing a stretching routine that'll help prevent injury? When you value your mental and physical preparation, you place tremendous importance on your performance.

In Rick Pitino's book, *The One-Day Contract*, the successful college basketball coach describes a core value that was based on the idea, "How would I approach today if I knew I had to earn tomorrow's contract?"

Hearing him say that, how would you approach your sport every day if tomorrow wasn't guaranteed? What about your approach or performance would change? Why not change it now and reap the benefits of being hungry to earn your keep at every practice and every game?

- **Team Values:** When a team decides to trade or let go of a superstar, fans are often left scratching their heads. Then, sometimes immediately, their team miraculously improves. It's no miracle. Even a team's best player can still be a hindrance if he or she isn't contributing to the team culture.

  In *Legacy*, best-selling author James Kerr describes many of the indoctrinated values that underpin the winningest franchise in sports history: the New Zealand All Blacks rugby club. One core value—*sweep the sheds*—involves the entire team cleaning the locker room from top-to-bottom after each match, whether home or away. The eldest players are the last to leave, making sure the locker room looks better than when they arrived.

Sweeping the sheds keeps each member levelheaded and reminds them that even after a victory in front of 50,000 fans, they're not above cleaning up after themselves. They don't expect any handouts from other teams, so they take care of each other. With the entitlement culture that many professionals live with today, it's refreshing some athletes still see themselves as human.

I witnessed this firsthand on a commercial flight when I accidentally sat in the wrong airplane seat after the Rugby Sevens tournament in Wellington, New Zealand, in 2015. My seat happened to belong to an All Blacks member who was flying from Wellington to Auckland to visit his girlfriend. He was very kind about the mishap. We joked about it and even took a photo commemorating the moment. He was down to earth. Just like you and me. Sweep the sheds.

Peak performance coach Brian Cain hosted an interview with University of Michigan head baseball coach Erik Bakich in late 2021. While other top baseball programs provide their players with endless supplies of gear from day one, Coach Bakich only issues a team shirt and a pair of sweats to the new guys. It's not that Michigan baseball is hurting for gear and equipment. He does this so every team member understands that entitlement is not an acceptable core value within the Michigan baseball program. No team will ever give Michigan baseball a win without them earning it. He instills this mindset with the issuance of team gear with the goal of it trickling onto the field.

What team values has your program established? If none, how can you begin to embody team values that'll raise the culture in your organization? You'll never be bigger than the team. Your sport will someday go on without you. Will you leave your jersey better than when you found it? Your values directly reflect the person you're striving to become.

Continue to draw the line in the sand for what you will and won't stand for. You'll be tested daily. Only you can decide if you'll pass the test. Like Tom Seaver, your values will change as you mature.

Continue to refine what's important to you. Having a strong *how* based on the right core values helps make tough decisions easier. Some people won't understand why you'll make the disciplined decisions you'll make. They don't have to understand now. Only you do.

When you finally get where you're striving to go and thrive, your destination will speak loudly on behalf of every decision you made during your journey.

Section III

SELF-COMPASSION

THE FUNDAMENTALS OF SELF-COMPASSION

Have you heard the term self-compassion? It probably sounds weak. Maybe soft. Especially in sports.

But before you skip this section, hang in there. If you've ever dealt with perfectionism or beat yourself up after making mistakes, you might just find self-compassion to be exactly what you're missing. So, what is self-compassion anyways?

In sports terms, self-compassion is being your best teammate. How much quicker would you rebound if—instead of beating yourself up every time you failed—you built yourself up the way a good teammate would?

You've been a good teammate before, right?

I asked that question to a new client, Conner, who was in his senior year of high school and struggling with the pressure of being a highly touted prospect in the upcoming Major League Baseball draft. As draft day neared, his backyard batting cage sessions turned from loose and relaxed to the pressure of Game 7 of the World Series with the bases loaded, two outs, and facing the best closer in baseball. He admitted there were times when if his first two swings didn't go well, he'd toss his bat and call himself every name in the book.

It didn't have to be that way. With everything at stake for him, baseball could still be fun. Baseball could still be the game he loved.

Connor was an ideal candidate for self-compassion. I asked him to describe a time when he was a good teammate. He told me about his good friend Charlie, who seldom struck out. At a wood bat tournament against some of the best competition in the state, though, Charlie struck out twice in a row. After he slammed his bat and helmet in the dugout, Connor went over, patted him on the back, and said, "Breathe, man. It happens. Let it go. You're still one of the best hitters I know."

I asked Connor why he did that.

"Because I wanted him to feel better."

"And why was that?"

A few seconds passed. "So he could move on and play like he always does," Connor responded.

Bingo.

Without knowing it, Connor was already a master of compassion. He'd hit all three components: mindfulness, common humanity, and kindness. When Connor told Charlie to breathe, he was helping his friend be mindful of the present moment so he could calm down and regain perspective. When Connor said striking out happens to everyone, he was talking about common humanity, that no one's perfect, and failure finds every athlete. When he reminded Charlie that he was one of the best hitters he knew, Connor's kindness was not only true but uplifting.

Connor grasped the value of being compassionate toward his teammate. It was time to turn that compassion inwards. It's easy to be compassionate toward someone else when he or she has failed. But when it's *you* feeling the heat of failure, it seems foreign to take a deep breath, tell yourself even the best fail often, and remind yourself you're still a good athlete and person despite having not gotten the job done.

In situations like these, you've likely beat yourself up, hoping it whips you into your best form. How well has that worked for you?

I asked Connor to close his eyes and imagine he was the one who struck out two times and was on the bench sulking. I then had him visualize his evil twin come sit next to him, push him, and tell him how bad he messed up and how terrible of a player he was. I let him sit in that for a bit to feel how those actions impacted his thoughts, emotions, and physiology.

Then, I had him reimagine the scene, but this time, I asked him to be the good teammate he'd been to Charlie. Connor visualized his good twin sitting next to him, leaning in shoulder to shoulder and encouraging him with words that would bring himself back to life. Afterward, I asked him which guy he wanted to be toward himself from now on. The evil twin he'd been to himself for who knows how long? Or the best teammate who would show up for him no matter what?

That's my definition of **mental toughness: showing up for yourself no matter what.**

Anyone can be good to themselves when things are going well. But can you be your greatest support system when things go south? Coaches are known to say some harsh things after you mess up. You can't count on them to pick you up.

It's great to have good teammates, and you will at times. But the sports world is a pyramid where everyone's looking out for themselves. You won't be able to depend on teammates to pick you up, especially those who might secretly be happy to see you fail.

You know who you can always depend on? Yourself. You are sometimes all you have. In those times, having a self-compassionate mindset is all you'll ever need.

Building yourself up may feel foreign now. But in this section, I'll help you train your inner coach to become the familiar voice and your inner critic to become the foreign voice.

By the end of this section, you'll see the value of self-compassion as a precursor to self-confidence. Let's begin with step one of self-compassion: mindfulness.

9

MINDFULNESS

It's not easy to move on from mistakes. But the opportunity to let go of them and begin again in the present moment is always available. The most important moment is when you recognize you're somewhere else besides right here, right now, where action is happening. This chapter will help you do that.

In sports, mindfulness is remembering to let go of what happened or might happen, to clearly see what's happening now without judgment. It's like balancing on one foot (present moment focus), losing your balance (distraction), and gently toe-tapping the ground to regain balance (mindfulness). All without beating yourself up (nonjudgmental awareness) for losing your balance in the first place.

Most athletes give less than 50 percent of their attention to the present moment. That means they miss about 50 percent of what happens during games. It's not their fault. It's not yours, either. The human brain is highly distractible due to *default brain mode*. Its only job is to keep you alive.

In sports, your brain's only job is to keep your athletic career alive. Your mind constantly shifts back and forth between the past and future, criticizing you for past mistakes and warning against future ones. No wonder it's so hard to be where your feet are.

THE WAR OF THE POUR

No performance is perfect. A bad call or mistake can taint the water glass of your mind with mental mud. Another mistake means more mud. Eventually, your mind becomes so muddy that you can't think clearly enough to see the game situation as it truly is. You're left with a murky version of what's happening. How can you expect to play well if you can't see clearly?

To get back to pure water—pure thinking—you have two choices: dump, rinse, and refill the glass with fresh water, *or* run your glass under a faucet until all the mud eventually filters out. Since you can't dump your brain, scrub it, and put it back in sparkly clean, only option two works. In order to battle the mud on auto-pour, you must constantly flush it out so you can see what's truly in front of you to make the right next move. It'll be a war of the pour between fresh and muddied thoughts.

Your mission as an athlete is to see the game situation as it truly is so you can make the right next move. This is where becoming a mindfully self-compassionate athlete is a game-changer. Let's break down this term.

Mindfulness, as defined by author Kristin Neff in her book, *Self-Compassion*, is "the clear seeing and nonjudgmental acceptance of what's occurring in the present moment. Facing up to reality, in other words."

Without mindfulness, you tend to over-identify with mistakes and self-sabotage your performance. But with mindfulness, you create a non-judgmental space between you and each failure so you can see it for what it is—an unfortunate moment in the past.

But mindfulness isn't enough. You still need follow-up action to return to playing well. That's where self-compassion comes in, which is a non-judgmental acceptance of what has happened with the desire to help you rebound.

THE MINDFULLY
SELF-COMPASSIONATE ATHLETE

Here are five steps to help you become a mindfully self-compassionate athlete, so you can see what's truly there and take the next right action with confidence. This rinse-and-repeat method will help you flush the mud so you can clearly see what's your right next move.

- ◆ Accept reality without judgment
- ◆ Be with your feelings
- ◆ Compassionately respond
- ◆ Discern what's still true
- ◆ Embrace the right next move

ACCEPT REALITY WITHOUT JUDGMENT

Your mind often makes a bigger deal out of mistakes than necessary. A mistake is genuinely just a mistake, but the meaning you attach to your failures can turn them into unnecessary drama. That's what happened to rookie first basemen Will Craig of the Pittsburg Pirates on May 27, 2021 versus the Chicago Cubs.

On a routine groundball hit to third base to end the game, the throw to first base was offline and pulled Craig off the bag to catch the ball. Instead of tagging the runner or stepping on first base for the force play to end the game, Craig bit the bait and chased the runner back towards home plate and overthrew the catcher. This led to a merry-go-round of errors that allowed the Cubs to come back and win the game. All because Will Craig momentarily forgot the fundamentals of baseball.

Here's how one media outlet described the play post-game, "This is definitely the worst play I've ever seen in baseball." Another source said, "... the biggest blunder of his baseball career went from a rundown choke into a running joke."

Here's Will Craig's original response a few days after his play went viral:

> "I replayed that probably 100-plus times in my head, exactly what happened. Of course, I'm going to end up on a blooper reel for the rest of my life, probably. I just keep moving forward with it, and I think the best way to do it is kind of just accept it head on. Don't deny it. Don't shy away from it. It happened."

This was a mature response. Yet, just a few weeks later when Will Craig was sent down to Triple-A, he asked for his release from the Pittsburg Pirates organization and signed with a team in the Korean Baseball Organization [KBO]. Here's his reason for requesting his release: "I feel like that play kind of defined me," Craig said. "I didn't want that to be the case. That's another thing that went into my decision to go over there [to the Korean Baseball Organization]. I need to almost start over in a way."

Will Craig, who was a gold glove first baseman in the minor leagues, allowed one defensive mishap to change his entire life and define his career. He has never played in the Major Leagues since. He believed he needed to take his baseball career across the world to turn the page when all he had to do was move on in his own mind.

The problem isn't the negative thoughts that arise after failing. When circumstances align for negative thoughts to arise—they'll arise. No one is immune to them. It's what you do with those negative thoughts that's important. How often do you magnify a mistake more than is necessary?

In *Self-Compassion*, Kristin Neff shares an equation from her mentor about the key to happiness:

Suffering = Pain x Resistance

She paraphrased him, saying, "The key to happiness is understanding that suffering is caused by *resisting* pain. We can't avoid pain in life, but we don't necessarily have to suffer because of that pain."

In sports, *suffering* is the negativity swirling around your head after failing. *Pain* can be a physical injury or something mental, like the embarrassment Will Craig felt after his fielding blunder. Pain often refers to something in the past that cannot be changed. *Resistance* is wishing things were different than how they are. The more you wish a situation is different than how it is, the more mental anguish you'll experience.

In sports terms, the equation is:

Negativity = Failure x Wishing Things Were Different

Failure is unavoidable, but negativity is optional. Mistakes will happen, but you don't have to get torn up about them. If you've ever said, "I should've . . ." or "If I could just . . ." that's wishing things were different than how they are. So, how do you change your resistance to failure?

Through acceptance.

Acceptance doesn't mean you don't care. It's not giving in to your emotions or the moment. It's actually the opposite of doing this. When you accept the present moment for what it is, you no longer ruminate over what can't be changed. You give yourself the freedom to let go and move on. Resistance keeps you stuck in the mud. Acceptance helps you flush what happened and move forward with clear vision.

The 2022 college baseball season was a week away, and Trevor was in the batting cage prepping for a team scrimmage. After several swings off the pitching machine, he felt so lost that he scrambled to find a reminder that he was still a good hitter. Confidence can be that fragile.

Remember, your two goals as an athlete are to see every moment as it truly is so you can make the right next move. Trevor was no longer seeing clearly. When he and I spoke the next day, he recalled how his mind spun after his batting practice.

"I was thinking, the season's a week away," he said. "How am I not ready? Why am I struggling off the machine? I feel like I'd never hit before in my life."

This wasn't some Little Leaguer struggling to put the bat on the ball.

This was a Division 1 athlete with high draft potential. If it can happen to someone a step away from the professional level, it can happen to anyone. Even you.

As Trevor and I reworked the situation, I shared the equation:

Negativity = Failure x Wishing Things Were Different.

He realized that had he paused to accept what really happened, he could've walked out of that batting cage unscathed, saying, "Well, that happened. That pitching machine is tougher than any pitcher I'll face. I'm fine."

The power of nonjudgmental acceptance allows you to see what really happened without blowing it out of proportion or over-identifying with it. I reminded Trevor that his batting practice session was simply what happened. It wasn't good. It wasn't bad. It was what it was. The less you resist failure, the quicker you can learn from it and move forward. The equation then shifts to:

Less Negativity = Failure x Less Resistance

When you learn to fully accept what happens without judging the result, your resistance level drops to zero. When this happens, you fully grasp that *wishing* things were different won't change what happened and won't prepare you for what's next. Full acceptance makes failure powerless over you. Mastery of this equation becomes:

Enjoyment = Failure x Full Acceptance

What can exist instead of negativity? Answer: enjoyment of every aspect of your sport no matter how things are going.

Trevor had distorted *a* round of batting practice into a *terrible* round. But when you enjoy your sport for everything it brings, a *bad* round softens to *a* round. This opens the door to examine failure from a place of kind curiosity rather than self-criticism. Your inner critic yells, "Why am I hitting so terribly?" without actually wanting an answer. But your inner coach asks, "How well am I seeing the ball?" and waits for an answer.

Self-criticism gets you nowhere. Kind curiosity gets you closer to where you want to be.

BE WITH YOUR FEELINGS

After you accept reality without judging yourself for what happened, a good portion of the emotional sting will subside. But not all of it. Most athletes don't want to sit with their feelings. They'd rather deny their emotions or sweep them under the rug. But ignoring how you feel will eventually lead to an emotional volcano.

Mindfulness gives your emotions ample space to be felt and heard. It's okay not to be positive all the time. Constantly putting on a happy face denies the reality that struggles exist. Struggles aren't all bad. They signify opportunities for improvement. If you never struggle, you can't fully appreciate overcoming adversity. Imagine a video game without any enemies or bosses. How fun would that be? The fun is in the fight.

At times, your emotions won't seem to move away from a bad game or play. Your inner critic wants to keep beating you up when you're down. But as you learned from Connor earlier, belittling yourself doesn't help. Not even a little. In that scenario, you're the one receiving the pain *and* the one dishing it out. That's double the negative impact, which is kind of silly, even sad. But to fixate on the failure more than the feeling it's causing you is detrimental to moving on from mistakes.

From now on, what if you cared more about your well-being than how badly you blew it? If you concentrated on being a good teammate to yourself after an error by checking in on yourself and asking how you're feeling, you become the helper and the one being helped. That's double the positive impact and double the rebound rate.

It's possible to feel something and not even know it. Sometimes we're so close to an intense emotion that we can't separate ourselves from it. Checking in creates the space necessary to find out how you're feeling without over-identifying with that emotion.

By holding your thoughts and feelings in mindful awareness, you hold the power. It's like taking a picture in selfie mode, holding it at arm's distance, and noticing (rather than judging) your current thoughts and emotional state. Emotions are what you feel. They're not who you are.

Trevor wasn't feeling lost after his battle in the batting cage. He *was* lost. At least in his own eyes. He was so blinded by doubt that he couldn't see the truth that he was still a good hitter, even though he had a common hitting moment. If he had paused to ask himself how he was feeling, he could've stopped the emotional boulder from picking up speed. That's the power of mindfulness.

Here's a sample inner dialogue that Trevor could've had after stepping out of the cage:

"Trevor, how you feeling?"

"Lost. I have no clue what I'm doing."

"Okay, take a deep breath. Are you lost . . . or are you feeling lost?"

"I guess I'm feeling lost."

"Is it true you're a terrible hitter and have no clue how to hit?"

"No. But I feel like it right now."

"Did you invite that feeling?"

"No."

"Then why believe an uninvited guest?"

"Ha-ha. True."

Mindfulness helps you realize that all undesired thoughts and emotions are just that: thoughts and emotions stopping by as uninvited guests who are free to leave anytime. Sometimes they'll go on their own. Sometimes they'll stick around. But since you didn't invite them, you don't have to entertain them. They'll only tell you lies, judge you, and criticize you. As you learn to hold your thoughts and feelings in mindful awareness, they become easier to slow down and examine without judgment.

The Achilles heel of mindfulness is that it stops short of providing you with solutions. But as self-compassion researcher Kristin Neff's says, "You can't heal what you can't feel." Mindfulness helps you know what you're feeling. Self-compassion helps you heal the feel.

COMPASSIONATELY RESPOND

Remember, mental toughness is showing up for yourself no matter what. The most mentally tough response to failure is, "What do I need right now?"

That may not sound macho, but macho is overrated and outdated. Having the wisdom to be steel when steel is needed and silk when silk is necessary is a true sign of mental toughness. Once you know how you feel, you have an idea of how to heal.

If you're angry, more anger won't improve the situation. But a little space could cool you off. If you're down, another verbal beatdown won't help. But placing a hand on your heart to soothe the pain might help. If the game is speeding up on you, playing faster isn't the solution, but a few deep breaths will slow your heart rate and quiet your mental state. If you need motivation, calling yourself lazy isn't going to get you moving. But an encouraging kick in the backside coupled with a reminder of your *why* will do the job.

It's not natural to want to help yourself because failing creates a disconnect between you and your ideal self. But it should be the opposite. As you learn to support yourself after mistakes, a stronger bond can be formed. Self-compassion's only goal is to heal what's hurting. Self-criticism's only goal is to hurt what's already hurting.

It takes courage to turn toward an emotion you wish you weren't feeling, but when you do so with mindful self-compassion, it's safe. When you focus on tending to your emotions instead of mulling over mistakes, you have a chance to bring healing to the feeling and move forward with confidence.

DISCERN WHAT'S STILL TRUE

After a mistake, the game situation and momentum have changed. But what's still true? Despite messing up, you're still a good player. If you struggle on offense, it's still true you can contribute on defense. If you're no longer in the game, it's still true you can support your teammates. If there's enough time, you can still help your team win. Discerning what's still true helps you rely on facts over fiction.

There's one place willing to give you the facts rather than fiction: the scoreboard. You may not always like what the scoreboard shows, but at least the score doesn't sugarcoat the truth. When you focus on what's still true instead of what went wrong, you have the clarity to make the right next move.

In Trevor Moawad's book, *It Takes What It Takes*, he describes a powerful strategy he coined called *shifting to neutral*. When a car is driving in reverse (negative), it must get to neutral before going forward (positive). In working with elite athletes who dealt with constant failure, he noticed positive thinking wasn't working. Getting to neutral was his alternative to positive thinking when positivity seemed unachievable. Shifting to neutral thinking involves:

- Owning what happened
- Knowing the past doesn't have to dictate what happens next
- Focusing on what is true about the situation without any influence from the past or future
- Setting unhelpful emotions aside momentarily to take action based on what is true

Moawad drives home this philosophy with an account from his well-known client, quarterback Russell Wilson. Down 19-7 to the Green Bay Packers in the 2014 NFC Championship game with a little over five minutes left, Russell Wilson (a Seattle Seahawk at the time) threw his fourth interception of the day. Bad timing to be having the worst game of his career.

After two burned timeouts and a stop by the defense, Russell Wilson got the ball back with just 3:30 remaining, still down 19-7. Here's my rendition of Trevor Moawad's story on how Russell Wilson was able to shift to neutral in the huddle . . .

> "Guys, I've sucked today. But that doesn't mean I'm going to keep sucking. Right now, we're down by two touchdowns. We need to score, get the ball back, and score again. We're still in this."

No positive speeches. No verbal beatdowns. Just facts. Just neutral. Wilson owned what had happened and described what needed to happen next for his team to have a chance to win.

It's not that Wilson wasn't emotional in those moments. It would be impossible not to feel something. He chose to set aside his feelings to focus on what needed to be done to have a chance to win. He focused on what was still true.

With the very arm that had betrayed him earlier, Russell Wilson threw two crisp passes downfield and used a quarterback sneak for a touchdown to cut the lead to 19-14 with 2:09 left on the clock. Then the Seahawks special teams successfully recovered an onside kick to get the ball back.

With new life, Wilson successfully threw to a tightly covered Luke Willson to get the ball downfield before Marshawn Lynch scored on a 24-yard run. A successful two-point conversion put the Seahawks up 22-19. Green Bay's field goal at the end of regulation sent the game into overtime, where the Seahawks ended up winning on a 35-yard pass from Wilson to Jermaine Kerse.

That's the power of neutral thinking.

After playing poorly most of the game, Russell Wilson still trusted his arm to get the job done when it mattered most. How? By shifting to neutral to see what was true about the situation—that despite how the game had gone—he was still one of the best quarterbacks in the league. Rather than let his emotions tell him how bad he was, he took the right next action each play. Right action cures emotion.

Emotions will cloud your vision. It's okay to feel emotions because you will anyway. That's why mindfulness is crucial to checking in, and self-compassion helps to heal the feel. But what if there's no time to sit in a feeling? A strategy taught by Trevor Moawad, which he called resisting emotions, entails putting aside whatever you're feeling for a time to do what needs to be done now. It's telling yourself, "Right now, I need to do. Not feel."

I do this when I golf. My graduate school mentor taught me to say, "That's interesting" after whatever happens on the golf course. If I hit a nice golf shot, I say, "That's interesting." If I hit a slice out-of-bounds, I say, "That's interesting."

In those moments, I feel something. Sometimes intensely. Yet, I know I can release those feelings when my round is over and I'm at my car changing out of my golf shoes. That way, I vent in an appropriate space after my scorecard is filled out with my best efforts. Usually, by then, the intensity of whatever I might have felt earlier is gone.

So, acknowledge what you're feeling, and if you don't have enough time to deal with how you feel, shift to neutral by setting aside your feelings with a deep breath and prioritize what you need to do based on what's still true.

Easy to say. Harder to do. But worth the effort.

EMBRACE THE RIGHT NEXT MOVE

After accepting what's still true, the last step is to embrace the right thing to do. The Navy SEALS abide by the motto *embrace the suck*. You won't always feel like doing what needs to be done. Emotions will whisper in your ear to throw a helmet or shove a Gatorade jug in frustration.

Although there are several possible responses to failure, there's only one correct one if you plan on becoming an elite athlete. It's up to you to embrace the right next move no matter what just happened. If you start with a deep breath, whatever needs to be done becomes clearer and more doable.

That's the step-by-step action plan for becoming a mindfully self-compassionate athlete. Sound weak? I don't think so.

To recap, here are your ABCDEs again:

- Accept reality without judgment
- Be with your feelings
- Compassionately respond
- Discern what's still true
- Embrace the right next move

Here's the abbreviated version for in-game performance:

1. What really happened?

2. How do I feel?

3. How do I heal?

4. What's still true?

5. What do I do?

As your mindfulness improves, you'll be able to enter every situation in neutral and see what's truly there rather than an inflated or deflated version of the truth. You'll also be equipped to support yourself with what you need in the moment.

There's no better way to build your confidence than by believing in yourself no matter what. Despite what's happened in the past, believe you are the right person for the moment.

10

COMMON HUMANITY

After failing, no one wants to hear, "Let it go. It happens to everyone."

But when taken to heart, those words remind us that even in our darkest moments, we're not alone. Whenever you mess up, know that countless others are going through or have already survived what you're experiencing or feeling. There's nothing new under the sun. It's only new to you.

The second component of self-compassion is *common humanity*, which is realizing you're human like everyone else. Self-compassion wouldn't be necessary if everything always went your way. But life and sports don't work in that manner. Every athlete fails. Not just you. Everyone struggles with negative thoughts. Not just you.

Some athletes are shocked when they struggle, as if something has gone terribly wrong. Sports are meant to be hard, and you are meant to be human. When things don't go perfectly to plan or you perform worse than expected, there's nothing wrong with you. You haven't gotten worse, even if last year's stats say so. Even the best in the world go through rough patches too.

No one wants to play poorly. That gets old really quick. But bad days are a part of every athlete's journey. It's actually your failures more than your successes that'll connect you and your teammates because everyone falls short at one time or another. You are not alone.

YOU ARE NOT ALONE

There's no lonelier feeling than messing up on a big stage. Retired NFL football player, Asante Cleveland, told me about his first game with the San Francisco 49ers. They were playing in Seattle against the Seahawks when the first-string tight end got injured.

At halftime, Asante's position coach told him he'd be playing the rest of the game. He was ready. On his first drive in the NFL, he played a crucial role in helping the 49ers score a touchdown. Pro football seemed easy. Then, on the next offensive drive, Asante was flagged for holding. Few fans pay attention when a flag is thrown. But for Asante, hearing his number called out over the loudspeaker in front of a Seattle fanbase known as the "12th Man" shattered whatever fairytale he might've had about playing in the NFL.

After the flag, he said he noticed how large the sellout crowd was and how loud they got. In a moment's time, he went from celebrating a touchdown with teammates to feeling completely alone amidst a packed stadium bearing down on him.

This is where the tunnel vision of self-criticism came in:

How could you cause that penalty?

No one else is getting penalties!

You're blowing your shot, rookie.

You'll probably get pulled from the game now.

Most athletes want to run and hide in these situations, but they can't. They end up listening to nerves urging them to play timidly going forward. "Don't let up" becomes "Don't mess up."

Had Asante known about self-compassion as it relates to common humanity, he could've taken a deep breath and reminded himself that he's human and mistakes will happen. He could've told himself that he was playing in his first professional game and that adversity would somehow find him—so why be shocked when it did?

A good mental reframe for Cleveland might have sounded like,

Everyone gets called for penalties. If I'm fortunate enough to have a long career, I'll have many more penalties called on me.

This self-compassionate response based on common humanity would've rebuilt his confidence and connection with himself rather than create greater division within. It would've given him the option to move on to the next play where he was most needed.

That's the power of common humanity. Mistakes happen, and they happen to everyone. No athlete is perfect. When you realize others go through what you experience, it helps soften the sting when you make a mistake on the field.

SELF-PITY VS. SELF-COMPASSION

There's a natural inclination to feel sorry for yourself when things don't go as planned. Self-pity fixates on how unlucky you are and disconnects you from others by convincing yourself that no one could possibly relate to what you're going through. Self-pity acts like quicksand, pulling you further into the pits of lonely despair where teammates, coaches, and parents can't rescue you.

Common humanity does the opposite by acknowledging that hard times and unfair circumstances happen to every athlete. But in this particular moment, it's happening to you. That's sports. That's life. Self-compassionate athletes find comfort in knowing others have gone through what they're going through and come out stronger for it.

Self-pity begs, *Why me?* Self-compassion asks, *Why not me?*

Why are you so special that you don't need to earn your starting spot every day? Why shouldn't you experience failure, bad luck, setbacks, injuries, or unfavorable calls? When you know these circumstances happen to every athlete, it makes them easier to digest and move on from when they happen to you.

A common frustration among baseball pitchers is defensive errors behind them. I'm quick to ask, "Do any other pitchers deal with this?" which usually gets a laugh. I remind them that there's even a designated spot on the scoreboard for errors. In other sports, it shouldn't surprise you when your shots aren't dropping or goals are getting scored on you. Since failure happens to the best of the best . . . it'll happen to you.

When you believe your performance is supposed to go a certain way, you set yourself up for a major downfall when it doesn't. Remember, there's an opponent across from you who wants the same thing you do. Only one of you can have it. Even in golf, the course is set up to challenge your every fiber. There are infinite possibilities for things not to go as planned. So why does it come as a shock when how you perform doesn't align with how you drew it up in your mind?

But when you buy into the perspective of *why not me,* you gain the wisdom to own what's yours and can maintain a sense of common humanity that not everything has to go your way in order for you to succeed. Common humanity even affords you to have a sense of humor when appropriate, because, sometimes you can do everything right and still not be rewarded. Sometimes all you can do is smile—knowing you did your job.

You signed up for a career of struggle. When adversity strikes, you can throw a pity party, or you can find common ground with every other athlete who's been through what you're going through. Self-pity narrows your vision down to you. Self-compassion opens your eyes to what's common to all athletes. Which perspective will help you rebound best and feel like you belong?

THE NEED TO BELONG

You may think you train hard to separate yourself from the rest, but in reality, you train hard to fit in where you want to belong. We all crave belonging. It's a basic human need. Nothing feels better than the connection formed through high fives and dog piles when you're able to contribute to your team's success. Few things are more isolating than that lonely walk back to the bench with your head down, feeling like you let your team down.

Without bonding with others, it's hard to feel comfortable, confident, desired, or happy. It's possible to feel like you don't belong even when surrounded by teammates. A client of mine expressed her dislike for attending college camps and told me why she refuses to attend.

"The girls at these camps are just in it for themselves," she said. "They think they're so good just because they're from SoCal. And if you don't know anyone, it's really awkward because no one's inviting you to join their little buddy club. They don't make it easy to feel welcome or have fun. So I don't go."

This is pretty common across all sports. The main focus of attending camps and showcases is to be seen by the right people who can offer you the chance to play at the next level. It's easy to feel isolated and alone when everyone is focused on themselves and their performance. The ironic part is that everyone's in the same boat. Having the awareness that everyone is chasing the same dream should bring a sense of togetherness, but it never does. When you understand everyone wants to be seen and be signed—but there's a scarcity for spots—it'll help you understand why some athletes act the way they act in mistreating or excluding you.

No matter what, people want to feel connected and feel a sense of security that even when things go wrong, at least they still belong. If you can't count on others to accept you for who you are, a good relationship with yourself will be your greatest support system that's always available.

THE COMPARISON TRAP

You will compare yourself to others. That's natural to do. Showcases, combines, and college camps are designed to evaluate players. But these events can be confidence killers for athletes who struggle when comparing themselves to equal or higher talent. Since comparisons are going to happen, let's make the most of them so your believing remains high no matter your competition.

SELF-ESTEEM VS. SELF-COMPASSION

High self-esteem was once thought to be the solution to low self-confidence. If you just thought highly enough of yourself, you could believe in yourself. While the heart behind having high self-esteem is good, the concept is quite flawed as several unanticipated consequences spring from trying to maintain high self-esteem:

- The constant need to see yourself in a positive light means you must see others in a negative light
- A developing sense of arrogance or narcissism (self-obsessed)
- Blaming others instead of taking responsibility
- Making excuses and lying to yourself when things don't go as planned
- Needing to be perfect

Self-esteem requires constant comparisons and asking, "How am I doing compared to others? Am I doing enough?" Self-compassion focuses on supporting you and asks, "What do I need right now?"

Phrases like "Somewhere, someone's outworking you" are self-esteem killers because no matter how much effort you put in, if someone's outworking you, how are you ever supposed to feel good about your work ethic?

Self-compassion doesn't require you to be better than everyone or belittle anyone to feel good about yourself. It acknowledges the truth that others can be good along with you. Self-compassion says you don't always have to be the best—and won't. It allows you to be genuinely happy for others when they succeed without the backlash of feeling like a failure.

APPRECIATING OTHERS' SUCCESS AND SKILLS

In 2021, I had several tough phone calls with high school seniors awaiting athletic scholarship offers. Time seemed to be running out to sign their letters of intent, and their friends were committing to teams all over the country. Some clients admitted they couldn't be truly happy for anyone else until they secured their own offers. Sure, they'd congratulate friends and teammates on social media, but inside were jealous, bitter, and frustrated. Those feelings are natural and human.

Are you genuinely happy for others when they succeed? Success for others doesn't have to equal failure for you. It's okay to be happy when others get what they worked hard to earn. Seeing someone of similar caliber obtain what you want can help you maintain hope that it's possible for you, too. Remember, everyone's striving for the same goal, so why not be happy for those close to you when they get what they earned?

When you magnify someone's strengths, it knocks your normalcy down a peg. Consider this self-talk:

That girl is fast, so I must be slow.

That guy throws 90 with movement, so my 83-mile-per-hour straight fastball won't get the job done.

That guy is six feet, five inches and I'm not even six-foot. How am I supposed to get noticed?

A great way to maintain your believing is to admire other players' gifts and talents. That way, you're not left feeling inferior as a person or player. To be a good player among other good players is a privilege, not a threat.

I loved playing against the best because I felt I belonged right there with them, but instead of appreciating their talent, I became envious and saw them as the enemy. Four comparisons killed my confidence as a baseball player: bigger calves, bigger forearms, fielders who threw a heavy ball, and hitters who seemed to have the ball jump off their bat.

I allowed myself to be intimidated by these qualities that are often synonymous with Major Leaguers because I possessed none of them. To me, these ballplayers were more desirable to scouts, and I was convinced they belonged to a fraternity to which I would never be welcome. The more I valued their physique and their abilities, the less I appreciated mine. *If that's what it takes to make it, I've got no chance.* But it wasn't true. I was a top high school player in my area in Southern California and was eventually recruited by a D-1 school. Yet, I couldn't appreciate my abilities because I was too focused on what I didn't have.

Maybe you've experienced something similar?

You don't have to like the way someone plays or overly applaud them after beating you. But you don't have to see them as the enemy or bad mouth them either. It's a sign of maturity when you respect a worthy opponent without viewing yourself in a negative light. Keep this thought in mind: It's possible for you *and* your competition to be good. Then you can repurpose your energy on getting better instead of being bitter.

When you feel the need to be better than everyone or be seen in a positive light, you'll feel threatened every time others perform well or better than you. It's not fun faking happiness for teammates when the glory falls on them. But when you're genuinely happy for them— because you understand their success doesn't necessarily ruin your life or your career—it's easier to feel connected, stay confident, and bask in the glory together.

SOCIAL MEDIA COMPARISON TRAP

Carter was a high school freshman baseball player who texted me this message: "I'd like to talk about learning to trust the process. I feel like I'm struggling with being patient in how I develop as a player compared to others."

Carter was following several high school phenoms his age on social media who'd already verbally committed to top baseball colleges by their *freshman* year. Their Instagram reels showed them throwing low nineties when most kids Carter's age throw in the high seventies. Carter was measuring himself against the top 1 percent in his age group. How often do you think he closed his social media feeling encouraged?

My advice to every athlete is to delete all social media or at least take a break from it periodically to recalibrate your perspective. There's more to life than scrolling through Instagram and TikTok.

Since Carter chose to continue following these freshman phenoms, we discussed strategies on how to benefit from their posts. He began studying these pitchers' mechanics to improve his own throwing technique. He also realized that each post was showing him what the next level of baseball looked like and what was potentially possible. These were ways he could be encouraged rather than discouraged when measuring himself against what he saw on social media. How about you? Does surfing social media motivate or deflate you?

Beware: social media is a dangerous place for comparisons. Athletes post clips to get scouted or to show off. There's nothing wrong with that. Where things go wrong is when you start comparing your actual self to their edited-to-perfection posts. You're staring at their highlights without their shortcomings. No matter how good someone looks online, their lives and sports careers are never as glamorous as they appear.

Every time you check social media or search what players college coaches are following, it reminds you how far behind you are and can kill your motivation. If you enjoy torture, keep scrolling until your day is ruined. Just know this: these people aren't thinking about you, so why devote so much energy to them? Consider pressing the unfollow button and remember no one's life is as perfect as they present it to be. If you do press the unfollow button, you'll be free to focus on closing the athletic gap between you and them.

When Carter got frustrated seeing someone his age so far ahead of him in ability, it made him want to be that good now. His impatience led to frustration. It's only human to want to be better than how you currently are. But you can only be who you are today and work hard to become better tomorrow. You have to build your abilities brick by brick day by day.

Trolling other athletes can tempt you to lose faith in your process. Remember, thinking too highly of others often makes you think less of yourself. If you find yourself jealous of others based on their social media account, I can promise you'll find that their lives aren't as great as they make them out to be.

That said, social media comparisons are not all bad. They can help you know where you stand against the competition and reveal what the next level looks like. Take whatever positives you can from others to speed up your learning curve while reminding yourself that you're not there *yet*.

COMPARED TO WHAT?

During rough patches, it's tempting to feel like everyone else is having success and fun all the time. It can seem like you're always behind in the count, getting guarded by the other team's best player, or getting singled out by the officials. It's easy to feel like you're having a really hard time . . . until you ask yourself, *compared to what?*

Jill was fifty when her father passed away. Understandably, her world was rocked and life felt empty for her without his presence. For fifty years, her dad was her source of wisdom, love, and support. Then he was gone. That's a hard concept to grasp for anyone. Amidst her grieving, a chance encounter changed Jill's entire perspective.

One day while standing in line at the grocery store, Jill met a man whose wife—a mother of four—had just passed away from COVID-19. That mother was fifty years old just like Jill. The man told her that his oldest child was twenty and the youngest was eight.

When Jill returned to her car, she realized the oldest of those kids only had their mother for twenty years and the youngest for just eight. Immediately, her perspective changed from how unfair it was to have her dad for fifty years to how incredibly fortunate she had been to have her dad for that long.

On a much lesser scale, another client of mine had to forego her high school senior trip to a tropical island to attend a mandatory conditioning camp for her Division 1 team. I reminded her how quickly any of her friends would skip a week-long vacation for a chance to compete at the Division 1 level for the next four years. I also told her that it wasn't a sacrifice she was making—it was a choice.

What in your life or career seems unfair or unlucky, but with proper perspective, makes you fortunate or favored? Do you think you're unlucky? If so, compared to what?

WHO CARES WHAT OTHERS THINK

There are few greater distractions than caring what others think. This goes back to the cognitive distortion *mind reading*. The fact is, unless someone genuinely tells you their opinion, you're left wasting mental energy trying to guess what they think of you. A female client would often say to me during our gym workouts, "I grunt and make all these noises doing body weight work. I'm embarrassing."

"Why is everyone here?" I'd ask.

"To get stronger."

"Okay. So, if you weren't grunting and working hard, then you could be concerned. Everyone here's worried about getting through their own workout. They're not worried about you . . . and if they are, that's their battle."

Everyone will have an opinion. That doesn't mean you should concern yourself with any of them. The peace of mind in not caring what others think gives you the freedom to be a human, capable of success or failure anytime you perform. Be you. If others don't like it, it's their problem. But if you chase everyone else's opinions and standards, you'll burn out and lose joy for your sport. Don't shrink your efforts because you think you look foolish.

Professional baseball pitcher Trevor Bauer never shied away from being himself.[2] His pre-game arm care routines were so different from the Arizona Diamondback protocols that he had trouble fitting in and was traded to Cleveland.

In Cleveland, he blossomed into one of baseball's most dominate pitchers. How? While everyone else continued to use traditional pitching

---

2   I know very well that Trevor Bauer was investigated for sexual assault allegations made against him and was suspended by Major League Baseball.

methods, Bauer took to technology and pitching analytics to maximize his potential and become arguably the best pitcher in baseball. Today, every MLB organization is on board the technology train.

Bryson DeChambeau is the Trevor Bauer of golf. He retooled his entire game based on analytics. Despite injuries, he has become one of the best golfers in the world, including winning the 2020 U.S. Open. Like Bauer, he's received his share of negative press from a sport known more for tradition than transformation. He doesn't care.

If you're striving to become elite at your sport, you have to get comfortable with hearing negative opinions about you. If you're not hearing them, you don't matter yet. Negative opinions never feel good. But your drive to excel must be stronger than those opinions.

A quarter-inch can be the difference between success and failure. You don't have time or energy to waste on what other people think. There's a good chance people in the stands aren't paying you close attention anyways, and your competitors are lost in their own heads.

Failing in front of others will happen. It's unavoidable. When you remember your identity is not in your sport but in being human, it becomes easier to fail in front of others without it crushing your world.

People will have their opinions about you no matter what, so trying to be perfect in their eyes is a losing battle. When you detach from the fear of not being perfect, it unlocks your freedom to have fun playing the game you love.

Common humanity means everyone fails. Instead of thinking *Why me?*, start thinking *Why not me?* It'll make a world of difference in how you perform.

11

PRACTICING SELF-KINDNESS

The third component of self-compassion is kindness—which is your willingness to be nice to yourself when things aren't going your way. Being good to yourself is always available, no matter how you're playing. It's a choice and one worth making time and time again.

Justin was a Division 1 college baseball player entering his junior year. He'd just completed a summer wood bat league, which earned him an All-Star team selection and the attention of professional scouts. He'd always thrived as the underdog, but now Justin was expected to be a team leader with high draft potential in the upcoming MLB draft.

Scouts flooded his fall practices. The pressure and demands Justin put on himself to impress the scouts ended up backfiring, causing him to sabotage his draft stock by trying to do too much. I was introduced to him soon after his struggles began and was called upon to help him reset his perspective and performance.

For two months, we built a self-compassionate approach emphasizing self-kindness to combat his negative spirals when things weren't going his way. Justin went from beating himself up over the most minor things to embracing those situations with kindness and curiosity to learn from them. Near the end of fall scrimmages, I asked him what areas he felt he was still struggling with.

"Honestly, I'm still having a hard time dealing with failure."

I then shared with him my equation from earlier:

Negativity = Failure x Wishing Things Were Different

As he learned to accept failure as a recurring theme in baseball, he started experiencing the benefits of letting negative outcomes go and moving forward to the next play. I reminded him that scouts had already seen him succeed. Now they wanted to see how he dealt with failure. This equation became his ticket to enjoying every aspect of baseball, whether he was struggling or not.

Less negativity allowed him to be kind to himself and love himself no matter what, knowing everyone struggles at times. In his final week of Fall Ball, scouts got their last peek at him before winter break. Instead of dreading the possibility of failing in front of them, Justin told me this:

> All the self-love came together. There were sixteen scouts there, and it didn't faze me at all. Even when I struck out, I just walked back to the dugout. Didn't cuss at myself or nothing. It was crazy. Everything clicked at that moment.
>
> All my teammates make fun of me for being the self-love guy. That's fine. My coach always says there are five hundred guys on bar stools across America with their shoulda-woulda-coulda-didn'ts. They'll see me on TV one day and say, "I used to play with that guy. He was self-love guy."

For years, Justin demanded perfection from himself without allowing room for failure. When he came to grips with failure as being unavoidable, he began playing with a newfound freedom through a self-compassionate lens. Freedom to fail, freedom to succeed, freedom to improve, and freedom to have fun playing baseball all became new options. I asked Justin to recap how self-compassion impacted his approach to baseball:

"I give myself credit where credit is due. I acknowledge *every* positive. Before, if I didn't hit my expectations, I'd call myself every name in the book. Even when I reached them, I basically told myself, "Good, that's what you're supposed to do."

But now, even after a good swing, I'm my biggest fan. I tell myself, 'Great swing Justin. You're meant to do this.' I'm using my first name a lot, building my relationship with myself. I'm done riding the extremes of that performance roller coaster. Keeping things on an even keel. I ain't afraid to be a self-love guy. Giving myself hugs. That's a game-changer."

Self-kindness had become Justin's new self-confidence. His capacity for self-kindness had been there his entire life. He'd shown these qualities toward others but never turned them toward himself.

Maybe you haven't either. Kindness and compassion are built within you. Whether they've been lying dormant for ten years or ten minutes, they're ready to be tapped. All you have to do is start treating yourself the way you would a struggling teammate.

EVERY ATHLETE'S NEED FOR SELF-KINDNESS

Athletes who criticize themselves believe that's the best way to improve their performance. But it's not true and never been true. Unnecessary demands from parents, coaches, the media, and organizations train athletes to be their own harshest critics, and they're starting to crack.

In recent years, top-level performers like Simone Biles and Naomi Osaka have taken time away from their sport, drained from a sports culture that reminds them how they've failed, or worse—how they're not allowed to fail. Performers are revealing that the pressure and expectations they face on the field are a cakewalk compared to the internal demons they battle in private: namely, perfectionism, anxiety, depression, and suicidal thoughts.

The sports world tries to deny you your right to *not* be okay. But it *is* okay to *not* be okay. It's just not ideal to stay there. No one should have to hide their struggles or suffering. Everyone deserves support.

In a perfect sports world, your hard work translates into immediate success. Unfortunately, the sports world isn't perfect, and your hard work often goes unrewarded. How you relate to yourself during those times—whether with kindness or criticism—partially determines the length of your career and the amount of joy you experience.

Self-kindness provides the emotional support you need to remain committed to your dreams and the confidence you'll get there. As you've learned, self-compassion is showing up for yourself no matter what—the definition of true mental toughness. It's giving yourself a hug when you need a hug and a loving push when necessary

---

TWO SIDES OF SELF-COMPASSION

Consider running into a mother bear. Get near her cubs, and she'll rip your face off. Yet, in a relaxed context, she grooms, nurtures, and even plays with her cubs.

These are the two sides of the self-compassion coin: steel and silk. Most athletes are familiar with their steely side but are less comfortable activating their silky side. Utilizing steel when steel is needed and silk when silk is necessary will make self-compassion your new superpower.

SELF-COMPASSION AND STEEL

Self-compassion holds your long-term goals in mind as it pushes you to do the more challenging things and not settle for what's easy or immediate. The steel side of self-compassion demands you to take action to protect, provide, or motivate. This is the fierce side of the mother bear who will do anything to protect her young. Keep these bullet points in mind:

◆ **Protecting:** Safety is priority number one. You can't play to your potential when you don't feel safe or are being mistreated. Protecting yourself means saying no to any threats or uncomfortable situations. On the field, tap into that mother bear mode to protect what your opponent is trying to take. The more personal you make the moment, the fiercer your focus will be.

◆ **Providing:** Know your needs and say yes to them. Playing for a team that provides a safe environment to fail, learn, and succeed is paramount to your progress. Provide compliments when they're due and encouragement when you're struggling. Mentally give yourself a high-five often.

◆ **Motivating:** While criticism is a popular motivation tactic, it's actually the greatest confidence killer. No one gets tougher through criticism. That said, self-compassion isn't an excuse to let yourself off the hook. Naturally, you want what's best for you, and you can motivate through encouragement, emotional support, and understanding—and help yourself grow.

SELF-COMPASSION AND SILK

The silk side of self-compassion requires no action. It's simply you being there for yourself to comfort, soothe, or validate, like a supportive parent or friend hugging you after a tough game or exhausting victory. No judgments. No words. Just feeling what you're feeling. The silk side of the mother bear mode is just as necessary as the fierce side. Keep these bullet points in mind:

- ◆ **Comforting:** Support yourself with the uplifting words you'd share with a struggling friend or teammate to help them rebound.

- ◆ **Soothing:** Use physical touch, like placing a hand on your heart or thigh, to let yourself know you "feel" your pain. Physical contact provides a sense of warmth and connection to help you calm down and return to a desired playing state.

- ◆ **Validating:** To validate yourself is to see the situation for what it truly is and talk yourself through a situation with kindness rather than criticism. An injured athlete can quickly become discouraged when seeing her teammates get scouted by colleges while she's stuck doing simple drills to regain her form. She can validate her feelings by saying, "This sucks. I'm angry and jealous. That should be me who's getting scouted, but I know I'll have my chance."

Validation admits the moment sucks but that it won't last forever. It allows the proper time and space to digest and deal with the disappointment in a healthy way, which then provides a clear path for moving forward.

Activating your steel side or silk side starts by asking yourself, "What do I need right now?" Sometimes you'll be your only comfort. Other times you'll be your only motivation. As you learn to integrate both sides of self-compassion, you create an incredible force of steel and silk to dominate any situation.

BENEFITS OF BEING KIND TO YOURSELF

Confidence is great when you have it, but confidence has been known to abandon athletes when they need it most. Self-kindness is easier to manufacture than confidence when playing less than your best. Keep this in mind: the kinder you are toward yourself, the quicker your confidence will return.

The world is hard enough on you. The sports world is even harder. Every sport is specifically designed to make it as difficult as possible to get what you want. Sand traps on the golf course? Those are for you. Facing a nasty curveball? Crafted for you. A basketball hoop designed just a bit bigger than the ball? Yeah, that's there to increase the difficulty for you. Your opponent knows their only job is to stop you from getting what you want. With all that built-in adversity, beating yourself up won't add to your performance.

But self-kindness will.

THE PRISON OF PERFECTIONISM

While attending a mindset conference, I listened to a speaker open with this thought-provoking statement: "I'll give fifty dollars to anyone who can tell me the first step to breaking out of prison."

Several hands shot up with elaborate explanations, but all were wrong. Then another hand went up. "Is the first step to getting out of prison . . . realizing you're *in* prison?"

Bingo. Fifty bucks.

In sports, perfectionism is the most significant mental prison, home to almost everyone at some point in their careers. Perfectionism tricks you into thinking that what you've done isn't enough, that you should be better than you currently are, or that you should never fail. Once you're convinced perfection is required with no room for failure, you're handcuffed and sentenced to a career of heavy self-criticism, anxiety, and depression with no release date.

Alysha, a volleyball client, told me about a tournament in which she missed a block at the net, resulting in a point for the opponent. Her team captain turned to her and shouted, "There's no room for errors!"

Alysha mentally shut down. That's what perfectionism does. It demands constant success with no room for failure. The sad part is that most of us believe it.

Perfectionism does have its fine points. Athletes with perfectionistic tendencies show incredible determination and tenacity toward their goals. But when these high achievers allow who they are to be defined by what they do, making mistakes can be misinterpreted as being a failure in life. That's why it's so hard for some to admit they have flaws, mess up, or, heaven forbid, aren't the best player on the court. No wonder perfectionism is a leading cause of depression, anxiety, and suicide among athletes and the general population.

When perfectionism grips you, the fun and challenge of improvement are replaced with the fear and shame of not being perfect already. But perfection isn't a prerequisite, even if it acts that way. Perfection tells you that if a skill doesn't come easily to you right away, then you'll never get it. And for some, not being good enough translates to not being lovable or acceptable in the eyes of others.

Look at making mistakes as manure for growth. How boring would life be if you already had all the answers and were successful in everything you did? As good as Kobe Bryant was, he still failed plenty of times over the years. Yet he said he saw failure as an exciting chance to improve his craft rather than a source of shame.

If sports were easy, you wouldn't play or watch them for long. It's the little victories amidst the imperfection and mistakes that keep you coming back for more. Sports expose every fiber of your being in front of audiences poised to cheer or boo you. What could be more exhilarating?

So how does one escape perfection's prison? The first step is to realize you're in it and have the desire to get out.

FAIL HARDER

Gil was experiencing mental breakdowns from his skateboarding hobby. He told me that he felt like his mind was being hijacked.

Little did Gil know that he was a prisoner of perfectionism, listening to demands like, "If you don't land this kick-flip three straight times, something bad will happen." When he failed to meet perfection's standards, which was often, he would throw his skateboard in frustration.

I asked why he continued skateboarding if the sport brought him so much mental anguish. He said he liked skateboarding when landing all of his tricks. It was messing up at his tricks that he couldn't stand. In Gil's mind, he wasn't just failing at a hobby. It was personal. Failing at skateboarding meant he was a failure at life.

I reminded Gil that if he wanted to be good at skateboarding, he needed to put in the work. But that information didn't register with him. He expected to perform like Tony Hawk without Tony Hawk's work ethic.

Next, I asked him about the whole mind-hijacking thing and whether anything terrible had ever happened after failing to meet perfection's demands. He said no.

I used his response as a teaching moment to share that perfectionism is a good liar, but all hot air with no follow through on its threats. Once Gil was convinced nothing bad would happen if he failed, I gave him a challenge. I said, "The next time you're working on your tricks, I want you to fail thirty times before you throw your skateboard."

He looked confused. "So you want me to fail?"

"Not on purpose." I replied. "But when you do, I want you to keep a running tally. Can you do it?"

"I'll try."

A week passed, and Gil came back beaming about how skateboarding was fun again. The challenge helped him realize there was no need to fear failing. The heart behind the assignment was to get him to challenge his relationship with failure. Once he knew he didn't have to be perfect—and wouldn't be—he had the freedom to have fun even when he didn't land every trick. Gil had never known the thrill of small progress until he released himself from mental prison by accepting failure as unavoidable and progress as the best part of pursuing mastery.

I'd like to say Gil was completely healed after this, but perfectionism is slimy and finds different ways to sneak back into your life if you let it. I check in on Gil from time to time to make sure he's allowing himself the freedom to fail—because it's going to happen anyway.

FINDING HUMOR IN MISSED TAKES

Both of my sisters regularly send me bloopers from our favorite show, *The Office*. In essence, a blooper is a mistake. A missed take. I'm amazed how actors can laugh off their missed takes and regroup to eventually get the next take right. Do you think they dwell on their missed takes, or focus on getting it right the next time the director says, "Action"?

Humor is an excellent remedy to help you regroup from mistakes for your next opportunity. Otherwise, anger and frustration will kill your joy in the process of improvement. If you lack enjoyment and consistently leave games or practices disappointed in yourself, you may be suffering from perfectionism. If you're unsure, check your stress, anxiety, and depression levels after competitions. They'll clue you in on whether you're carrying burdens that no athlete should have to bear. When in doubt, add a little humor.

PERMISSION TO NOT HAVE TO BE PERFECT

The more time and effort you put into your craft, the more you expect perfection. Once perfection is entrenched as a belief, you imprison yourself to impossibly high standards with no allowance for failure. If unquestioned, perfectionism will persuade you to set your expectations so unattainably high that you'll be left disappointed no matter how well you play. That's what happened to Dillon.

Dillon was relying on his high school senior baseball season to earn a college scholarship after an injury ended a promising junior year. We met a few games into his senior season when he was struggling to hold onto his starting spot, let alone earn a scholarship. From our first conversation, I could tell he believed he needed to play flawlessly if he was going to earn a scholarship.

The quest for perfection will sink anyone's season.

Our talks hovered around the immense pressure he was placing on himself at practice and games to perform at a high level. He wanted to amaze everyone. Ironically, the more he focused on what others thought of him, the less he focused on seeing the baseball. He played horribly.

In his mind, failing in front of others meant *he* was a failure in their eyes. As the season went on and he continued to fall short of his expectations, he would lock himself in his room and ruminate over how bad he played that day, as if beating himself up could change what happened.

Even on the days he performed well by anyone else's standards, he couldn't be satisfied. Nothing was good enough, not if he hadn't won a coveted scholarship. That's the definition of perfectionism.

His anxiety before games, stress during games, and depression after games routinely killed any enjoyment Dillon once gained from baseball. He was carrying perfection's burden without knowing it. That's when I offered him a way to drop it all. Here's how our conversation played out:

> "Dillon, when's the last time you had a perfect practice or played a perfect game?"
>
> After some consideration, he answered, "Never."
>
> I leaned my ear toward him. "How often?"
>
> "Never," he said with a smile.
>
> "So why do you keep demanding perfection if it carries a 100 percent fail rate?"
>
> Through an embarrassed grin, he said, "Yeah. Makes sense."
>
> "And if you've never played perfectly, how many games have you messed up in?"
>
> "All of them."
>
> "So, if you know not everything will go your way, what's

more beneficial: expecting perfection or giving yourself permission to fail?"

He knew the answer but seemed to fight it. "The second one, I guess."

I nodded. "I know it sounds weird to be okay with failing, but since it's going to happen anyway, why not learn to accept when it does and give yourself the freedom to move on to the next play?"

"I think that would really help me."

"Heck yeah, it would!"

He sat up a bit in his chair. "I think I put so much pressure on myself to be perfect that all I'm thinking is, 'Don't mess this up.'"

"Sounds like you're having a good time out there."

Dillon laughed. "Not at all."

"Listen, everyone messes up. No one plays perfectly. If you think someone does, go ask him, and he'll give you a laundry list of ways he falls short."

"Yeah."

"And just so we're clear . . . giving yourself permission to fail isn't a free pass to not trying. It's meant to lift a mental burden. You can be aggressive again and take risks. It's fun being on the attack rather than on the run. When's the last time you had fun playing baseball?"

"It's been a while. Too long." Dillon took a deep breath to digest everything. "I get what you're saying. It's just hard to accept failure, I guess. If I keep failing, I know I won't play in college."

"I'm more concerned about now. If you keep falling

apart when things don't go perfectly, you'll finish second string on your high school team."

"True."

I had him stand up, close his eyes, and repeat after me, "I, Dillon, grant myself permission to fail . . . I, Dillon, give myself permission to be kind to myself . . . I, Dillon, grant myself the freedom to have fun again."

I then instructed Dillon to release his words like a mental brick and allow peace and relaxation to wash over him. He was free. For the moment at least.

In his final high school playoff game, his team was down 9-2 in the top of the sixth inning. Dillon came to the plate with the bases loaded. With two quick strikes on him—which would've sunk his confidence earlier in the season—he hit a grand slam to get the score to 9-6. His team continued the rally and eventually took the lead before losing in the bottom of the 7th.

After the game, I asked Dillon about his at-bat. "I've never been so focused in my life," he explained. "I wasn't thinking about how big the crowd was, my stats, or whether college scouts were watching. I wasn't worried about getting out. I wanted to help the team and concentrated on seeing the ball well. I was having fun and just happened to run into one."

Giving yourself the freedom to perform to your utmost abilities can set you free from a self-imposed mental prison you may be living in. It's up to you to realize if you're a prisoner of perfection and want to get out. If you want your sport to be fun again and to extend your career, embrace the fact that failure will happen every game. Since failure happens to all of us, there's no reason to fear it. Instead, learn from your failures, then move on to the next moment where your best is being requested. Remember, sports are meant to be hard, and you are meant to be human.

UNLOCKING YOUR MENTAL PRISON

Throughout the Self-Compassion section, you've been handed the tools to break out of prison through practicing mindfulness, common humanity, and self-kindness.

Mindfulness takes a non-judgmental look at any situation and sees it as it truly is, not better and not worse. Perfectionism will yell, "How could you let that ball go through your legs, you idiot?" and not care for an answer. Mindfulness will ask, "Why do you think that routine ground ball went through your legs? How can we fix it for next time?" These questions open the floor for a response so you can rebound with confidence and clarity.

Perfection leaves no room for errors and singles you out as the only one screwing up. Common humanity reminds you that you're human just like everyone else, bound to make errors and struggle. You're aware that even the best players struggle at times.

Perfectionism will call you every name in the book and never apologize. It will cut you down and strip your confidence. Self-kindness supplies you with a limitless amount of love and support so you can get back to playing with confidence.

The length and enjoyment of your career will heavily depend on your relationship with yourself. A relationship built on kindness is achievable. A relationship built on perfection is unattainable.

You never know where your career will go when it starts with self-compassion. Now that you're equipped to escape your own mental prison, it's time to build a vocabulary of victory. Your words have the power to make or break your career.

Section IV

VOCABULARY
OF VICTORY

12

VOCABULARY OF VICTORY

There's a popular saying in sports: "The battle is won or lost between the ears."

It's true. That battle is referring to your believing. The weapons of warfare are your words, which will be your greatest ally or worst enemy. The battle for your believing is winnable every time. This chapter will show you how.

THE POWER OF YOUR TONGUE

Like a small steering wheel that guides a massive cargo ship, your tongue directs the course of your entire career. Your tongue can also destroy your career like a forest fire set ablaze by a single spark. Look no further than ESPN, where loose words consistently cost players and coaches their careers and reputations.

Which will you train your tongue to do? Build or break your confidence? Help or hurt your career? The choice is yours to train your tongue to work for you. Otherwise, your tongue will naturally work against you.

THE DEPTH OF YOUR WORDS

When I was a kid, my family visited an area of California's High Sierra mountains with natural water slides that fed into deep potholes. My parents warned us to surface quickly so as not to get swept under. You can't always tell the depth of water by looking at the surface. The same goes for your words.

We've all heard that playground saying: "Sticks and stones may break my bones, but words will never hurt me." But nothing could be further from the truth. Broken bones heal naturally, but shattered confidence caused by jagged words takes far more effort to mend.

Remember the story about volleyball player Alysha, whose teammate yelled, "There's no room for errors"? To Alysha's team captain, those words might have been her way of showing leadership. But to Alysha, they were daggers that cut deep and caused her to mentally check out.

Many athletes spout out of their mouths without considering the impact of their words. Words can help or hurt on four levels:

- **Words for self:** Is your self-talk encouraging or discouraging?
- **Words from self:** Have you conditioned yourself to speak encouragingly or disparagingly?
- **Words for others:** Do your words build others up or tear them down?
- **Words from others:** Do you allow others' words to help or hurt you?

Every word you speak to yourself and others affects you for good or bad. You can learn to condition your words so that every word you say carries the impact you want and accomplishes what you intend.

TRAINING YOUR TONGUE

In the gym, training your body to meet the demands of your sport is crucial to peak performance. The goal in training your words is to condition your mind to think before you speak. This often results in speaking less but accomplishing more with what you say.

I once had a former client who had a reputation of saying whatever popped into his head. Despite his intellect, his words got him in trouble.

The wisest man who ever lived, King Solomon, said that even a fool is counted wise when he keeps his mouth shut (Proverbs 17:28). That's what conditioning your words will do. It'll give you the wisdom to know whether to speak, what to say, and when to say it so your words accomplish their purpose.

I believe that you can train your tongue in four ways: quality, quantity, integrity, and intention. Let's take a closer look at these:

QUALITY

Everything you eat and drink affects you. The quality of your nutrition determines the quality of your mental and physical state. When it comes to training your words, anything your eyes and ears digest also impacts how you think and perform.

The quality of your thought life will be determined by the quality of what you mentally entertain. What social media apps, TV shows, or movies are you watching? What caliber of conversations are you having? Remember: what flows in will flow out. Here's how to condition the quality of your words:

- **Front-load the hard work.** Someone's probably told you, "Watch your mouth." It's not bad advice. But it's putting the effort in the wrong place. Monitoring every word you say will leave you exhausted and unable to focus on what's important. The solution? Front-load the hard work. Instead of trying to manage everything that comes out, filter what comes in.

    You cannot control every thought that pops into your head, but you can control who you spend time with and what you watch on the internet, social media, or TV. When you consistently screen what you entertain, you front-load the hard work and won't have to worry about what comes out. The quality of your input determines the quality of your output. Like gravity, what's in your mind drops out of your mouth.

TRAINING FOR QUALITY

Draw a line down the middle of a piece of paper. Title one side "Treasure" and the other side "Trash." Then categorize everything you consistently watch and hear and your conversation topics with people. Consider both sides of your paper and ask yourself how each source impacts how you think and speak to yourself and others.

Decide what you want to do with each source—whether to treasure or trash it. The more trash you keep, the more trash you'll speak. The more treasure you hold, the more you'll have mental gold.

QUANTITY

When you improve the quality of your inputs, you may find the quantity of your words becoming less because you're not repeating drama and gossip from others. There's wisdom in talking less and doing more.

Why does a lumberjack sharpen a dull axe? To accomplish more by doing less. When you sharpen your words like a lumberjack sharpens his axe, your words will cut right to the point and accomplish far more with less effort.

- **Stop Saying Stupid Stuff.** In his book, *It Takes What it Takes*, Trevor Moawad shares a team rule he established with college football teams he worked with: *Stop saying stupid stuff.* The goal was to decrease the immature things athletes were saying without thinking. It's a great rule, but it's incomplete. It's impossible not to say stupid stuff if the majority of your input is stupidity. Changing the quality of your inputs decreases the quantity of worthless words. That transformation happens from the inside out.

I ate lunch with a former co-worker after not seeing her for over a year. About halfway through our meal, she asked, "Are you okay? You just don't seem like yourself. You used to be super funny and talk a lot more."

I was a bit offended before I realized what she was talking about. When we were co-workers, I took pride in my quick wit for a good laugh. But this person didn't know that I'd spent the last year of my life prioritizing my Christian faith by studying the Bible and surrounding myself with church friends. I had changed my inputs and my inputs had changed me. My friend was used to the old me who would say stupid stuff just to say stuff. The new me was thinking before speaking. I had learned to ask: *Is what I'm about to say beneficial? Is the topic we're discussing of value or useless gossip?*

My friend was witnessing tangible proof that I was conditioning my words by conditioning my heart.

TRAINING FOR QUANTITY

A great way to decrease the quantity of negative words is pausing before you speak and asking yourself, "Is what I'm about to say going to help or hurt?" Pick a particular day to consider how much garbage spews from your mouth. Tally up your trash and consider how you might stop saying stupid stuff moving forward.

As you mature towards a vocabulary of victory, you may find yourself speaking less and leaving fewer opportunities to harm yourself or others with your words. When in doubt, take time to consider your responses, or don't speak at all. On the field, nothing rattles an opponent more than not returning their trash talk. They'll get bored with you, knowing they're not going to get a rise out of you. When you're in a leadership or captain role, speaking less results in people listening *more*. If all you ever do is talk, people will shut down the second you speak.

INTEGRITY

Do your words work? As in, do they accomplish their goal when you speak?

- **Do the Harder Thing.** Some say to follow your heart. That's a terrible idea since emotions guide your heart. The only time following your heart is okay is when you've conditioned your words to tell you the right thing to do, despite how you feel.

  An excellent way to train for this is by doing the harder thing. When you have a dirty bowl, instead of placing it in the sink, train yourself to wash the bowl and your silverware. If someone else left a dirty dish behind, wash that too. When you're at the gym, train yourself to put away your equipment, wipe it down, *and* put away someone else's piece of equipment if they left it out.

  Do the harder thing. Then expect the mental benefits to carry over into your performance.

  Soon enough, you'll be at the gym by yourself, and after your last set, your mind will be conditioned to tell you, "Finish with some core work." This is your mind telling you to take positive action. If you do it, you're conditioning your mind to tell your body the right thing to do, which will pay off in games. When you need to take a deep breath to slow the moment, your mind will be trained to do so. Eventually, the harder thing becomes your norm while everyone else's mind is telling them to cut corners.

  The opposite of doing the harder thing is making promises you can't keep. It's better not to make a promise than to make one and not fulfill it. If you set goals to go to bed at a certain time, eat a certain way, or arrive at practice at a certain time and don't, your words lose credibility, authority, and integrity. The unconditioned mind and body are always looking for the easy way out, and if you give them an out, they'll take it.

When I'm standing on a tee box, waggling my golf club, I tell myself what to do by telling the ball where to go. When you tell yourself what to do, and do it consistently, you give yourself another option for success when you find yourself getting mechanical. Tell your body what you want it to do. When properly trained, the body will shut off think mode and turn on trust mode.

If you want to be trustworthy, follow through on what you say. Your body is an excellent bull crap meter. If your words carry no authority, your body won't listen. Neither will anyone else. Your words gain power and integrity every time you do what you say.

TRAINING YOUR INTEGRITY

If you want your words to work, consistently train your body to obey them. Tell your body what to do. If you want it to relax, do fifty jumping jacks to raise your heart rate, then do breathing exercises as you tell your body, in a calming tone, to relax. Start small, then increase the demand as you train your body to listen.

INTENT

I remember finding out through social media that one of my professional baseball clients, a pitcher, was the last player sent down to minor league camp on the final day of spring training in 2021. I was as shocked as he was. He'd done everything within his control to head north with his Major League team and had the spring training results to back it up.

Despite performing better than a few other guys in the same predicament, he had minor league options left on his contract and the other pitchers did not. At that level, many times it comes down to business decisions. That doesn't mean my client didn't stay up all night replaying every pitch he threw in spring training, trying to figure out why he was still in a Florida hotel at extended spring training when he should've been on a chartered plane with the rest of the Major League players.

The very same week, I received a phone call from a high school athlete who, through tears and a running nose, revealed she hadn't made the high school freshman golf team. This girl had an unmatched work ethic, especially during the pandemic when many athletes chose laziness over hard work.

Whether it's failing to make a Major League roster or a high school freshman team, hearing *you're not good enough right now* is never easy. If you're fortunate enough to play your sport long enough, there will be bad beats that'll keep you up at night. During these sleepless nights, the washing machine of verbal and emotional warfare tumbling around your head can take you from confusion to anger to feeling overwhelmed.

In those dark moments, your heart needs words of comfort and direction. The place we often go is inward. But contrary to popular belief, the more you mull things over within yourself, the darker the hole of self-doubt gets. If there's nothing good there now, searching deeper isn't going to help.

- **The Power of I Will.** When you're ready to stop the mental spin cycle, there's great power in "I will." Coupled with a deep breath, put this two-word powerhouse up against any army of defeating dialogue, and *I will* wins out every time because action cures emotions.

  By the end of your *I Will* campaign, your negative dialogue should be quenched or at least quieted so that you can get some much-needed rest for your exciting comeback journey. Even if you started today off with bad news or a bad performance, by willing yourself forward with the intent to be better from it, you can be at peace, encouraged, and excited about what's next. Instead of searching inward into the dark abyss, here are some new directions to look towards:

TRAINING YOUR INTENT

I Will Look Backward: at my past accomplishments to remind myself of my best performances. I will meditate on my moments of glory and remind myself I'm still just as capable today. I will look back on recent games and consider what I did well, what I could have done better, and how I can improve moving forward.

The Major League manager of my client who just missed making the Major League roster told my client he needed to work on his pitch efficiency to be effective at the next level. My client had two choices: wallow and hide or swallow his pride and get to work on his pitch efficiency. He chose the latter, reached the big leagues before the All-Star break, and remained there for the rest of the season.

I Will Look Upward: to God and vent to Him all of my frustrations and sorrows because He can bear them better than I can, and He will never, ever leave my side.

I Will Look Outward: If God isn't your thing, call on a trusted mentor who will give you a listening ear. Or journal. No matter what, find an outlet to purge pent-up thoughts and emotions so you can find rest and heal. Empty your mental bowl so it's useful again.

I Will Look Forward: I will feel my emotions until they've run their course or until I say it's time to put the past to rest. Then, I will vow to move forward without those mental bricks slowing me down.

I Will Look Downward: at my feet. Movement is healing and motivating. What is the next step I must take to get where I want to go? I may not feel like taking that step, but I will take it anyway. Then another.

SYNCHRONIZED LIVING

If I point to an apple tree and ask you what kind of tree it is, how would you know it's an apple tree? Answer: by its fruit.

If I were to ask someone what kind of person you are, how would they know? By your words and actions. Remember, what's in your heart will come out of your mouth. If you're bitter, you'll speak bitterness. If you're confident, you'll speak and exude confidence. If you ever want to know the quality of someone's thought life—just listen. They'll let you know.

You are the first person impacted by your words. If you find yourself speaking death to even one person, that's one person too many. What do you want your words to accomplish?

- ◆ *Text:* What's the right message?
- ◆ *Tone:* How should it be said?
- ◆ *Timing:* When's the best time to say it?

Your words have the ability to make or break your performance. The battle is truly won or lost between your ears. When you condition your vocabulary for victory by training for quality, quantity, integrity, and intent, you'll consistently win the battle of believing.

YOUR WORDS ARE YOUR REPUTATION

Warren Buffet, one of the wealthiest people in the world, said one time, "It takes twenty years to build a reputation and five minutes to ruin it. If you think about that, you'll do things differently."

In regard to developing a vocabulary of victory, social media is a dangerous game offering more ways to hurt you than help you. You won't get in trouble by saying nothing. The best way to say nothing on social media is not to use it. But I understand that deleting social media is likely out of the question—for you and for me. Because of that, this section will help you use social media *for* you rather than against you.

Social media is like a torch: it can illuminate or incinerate. Every comment and photo you've ever posted tells the world what kind of person you are. You post it, you own it. Everything you say, post, and do will be scrutinized by coaches, organizations, and fans. They want to know if you'll represent their program or organization well. If you make it big, somebody will dig up your posts from the past and use them to ruin your reputation.

What this means is that the world will form an opinion of you via social media long before they ever meet the real you. I like this strategy from Jim Afremow's book, *The Young Champion's Mind,* for ensuring your social media illuminates rather than incinerates you:

Jim wants you to think of three character traits you want to be known by. Write them down here or on a sheet of paper.

....

....

....

Next, make these three traits the home screen background on your phone. Everything you comment on or post to social media needs to project these three character traits.

People are going to judge you by your social media. You can either leave their judgments to chance, or you can take control by using social media as a billboard for your own personal brand.

SOCIAL MEDIA FOR MOTIVATION

After winning his fourth NBA championship with the Golden State Warriors in June 2022, Klay Thompson, who usually remains quite reserved, spoke his mind about a tweet from a member of the Memphis Grizzlies that had been fueling him.

Earlier in the season, a Grizzlies player wrote a tweet that said, "Strength in numbers," after the Memphis team defeated Golden State 123-95 in a blowout win. It was also a night when Steph Curry, Draymond Green, and Klay Thompson didn't play. The fact that the Grizzlies' player was mocking them by using the Golden State Warriors team slogan felt like he was pouring salt on an open wound to Klay.

From the NBA championship media room, Klay Thompson shared how mad the tweet had made him. But rather than fight back on social media at the time, he channeled the mocking tweet as motivation to push him and his teammates to finish the season on top.

The Golden State Warriors had the last laugh. If you're going to use social media, use it for fuel rather than fire.

IN-PERSON INTERVIEWS

Remember, people will learn everything they need to know about you through your words and actions, and nowhere do coaches and scouts get a better seat than when they're interviewing you before signing you or offering you a scholarship. The following bullet points will help you sharpen your interview skills and show your best when speaking to recruiters, coaches, or the media:

- Use his or her last name, as in "Hello, Coach Smith" or "Nice to meet you, Coach Jones."

- Use a firm handshake.

- Hold strong eye contact.

- Smile as though you enjoy your sport.

- Don't chew gum while being interviewed.

- Give them your full attention.

- Let your body language and tone of voice exude confidence.

- Your answers matter. Think before you speak.

- Be honest and smart about what you say.

- Answer controversial questions with: "I don't know much about that . . ." or "What I'm focused on now is getting ready for the next game" or "That's not up to me to decide."

- If questions are unclear, say, "I'm not sure I understand the question . . ." so they can rephrase or explain what they're really after.

- If you're being interviewed after a victory, allow yourself to be excited. Doing so shows others how much fun you had. Dish out credit to others, too.

- Own mistakes. Share triumphs.

Whether it's being part of in-person interviews or engaging in social media, both take forethought and practice. Leaving your reputation to chance is a sure ticket to misrepresenting who you are and what you bring to your sport. Your reputation will be built on one interview, one post, and one interaction at a time. Be especially careful with social media posts because those are impossible to take back. Build wisely and strategically.

Finally, you won't always win the battle on the field, but you can always win the battle of believing. It starts with building a vocabulary of victory. Prioritize your words by training your tongue for quality, quantity, integrity, and intent. That way, you'll give yourself the best chance of winning the battle between your ears and the one on the field.

Section V

VISION

13

VISION

"I can tell you I wouldn't be where I am now if I hadn't seen myself wearing a big-league uniform long before it happened. I believe in the power of dreams."

—Alex Rodriguez, former Major League Baseball Player

In the late 1980s, actor Jim Carrey was broke and relatively unknown. Every night, he would cruise up Mulholland Drive to overlook Los Angeles and visualize becoming a Hollywood star. At the time, little evidence of a successful future existed beyond a few directors and close friends telling Carrey that he was a talented actor. Yet no matter how many rejections the day brought, he still visualized his life playing out successfully to remind himself that his talent and commitment would pay off.

In 1992, he wrote himself a $10 million check for "Acting Services Rendered." He signed the check and dated it for Thanksgiving 1995, then folded it in his wallet. Then Carrey continued grinding away at his craft, never forgetting his dream or that eight-figure check he wrote to himself.

A few years later, just before Thanksgiving 1995, he learned he'd landed a lead role in a movie called *Dumb and Dumber*. His paycheck? Ten million dollars. Jim Carrey saw a clear vision for himself. Believed it. And acted on it.

Will this happen for everyone? No. But Carrey's story serves as a fundamental blueprint if you have huge aspirations and little momentum. He woke up hungry to chase his dreams and ended his evenings visualizing his desired future until he made it a reality. Do you wake up hungry to chase your dreams? Do you end your nights visualizing playing in packed stadiums? If not, why not? How will you ever attain what you can't see in your brain?

No one will believe in your vision until you do. Once you do, your mind and body will respond with drive and purpose. Today, give everything you have to get a little better. A little closer. That's what vision provides you with—fuel and faith to pursue what you want.

VISUALIZATION

Close your eyes and imagine biting into a big juicy lemon.

What did your face do? How did your mouth react? You probably winced at the thought of biting a lemon, and your mouth might've started to pucker. That's the power mental imagery has on your mind and body. Your mind is a visualization machine willing to show you anything or take you anywhere in a moment's time.

Are you using visualization for or against you? Many athletes allow their imaginations to dwell on how bad things can go, which can result in lost motivation. But the Jim Carrey route—using your imagination to fuel the life and career you desire—is a great way to pursue what matters most to you.

When athletes discuss how little playing time or practice repetitions they're getting, I ask them how many mental reps they're taking. You may only get so many opportunities in a game or practice, but mental reps can be limitless. Visualization is as real as you want to make it. Your mind and body react to mental reps the same way they respond to biting a lemon. Motor neurons in the brain fire as if you were actually performing. So whether you want to ingrain a new technique, routine, or just stay sharp while injured, whatever you imagine gets reinforced in your motor patterns.

You are the director of your mental movies. You can view yourself performing from any angle and perspective you want. You can freeze-frame, rewind, slow down, or speed up. Should you only visualize playing perfectly? No. Not everything will go your way, so why not practice rebounding from mistakes? There is tremendous value in seeing yourself struggle and turning your own performance around. In actual competition, you'll do what you visualized. You can build confidence in any area of your game by imagining yourself repeatedly doing a particular skill well.

BUILDING A DAILY VISUALIZATION ROUTINE

When you know what you want, you can confidently go after it. Until then, you're only throwing darts in a dark room, hoping to hit the bull's-eye.

The term *dirt dive* comes from the Navy SEALs who visualize their training and missions. Dirt diving starts with how you want things to go. Then, how to rebound when things go wrong. Your day will never go as planned. So why not prepare for the unpredictable so you remain confident in the face of chaos? Here's a template for daily visualizations:

Big Picture:

- ◆ What vision do you have for your career? See it. Soak it in.

Morning Wake-Up Dirt Dive

- ◆ How do you want your day to go?
- ◆ What will likely go wrong?
- ◆ How can you best prepare for what may go wrong?

Game Day/Workout/Practice Dirt Dive

- ◆ How do you want to perform today?

- What will likely go wrong?
- How can you best prepare for what may go wrong?

Bedtime Stories

- How do you portray yourself in the stories you tell yourself before bed?
- What obstacles do you face as the main character?
- How do you overcome those obstacles to be victorious?

When you become the hero in your life by visualizing yourself experiencing success, you build trust between your mind and body that you are the right person for the situation. If the majority of the stories you tell yourself are negative, you unconsciously ingrain the wrong messages that will wreak havoc on your performance. Choose to use your mind rather than be used by it.

PLAYING OUT OF YOUR MIND

Sports psychologist Dr. Bob Rotella explains that skills are developed through conscious effort but eventually become automatic subconscious actions. For instance, when you first learned to text message, it took a conscious effort to type letter by letter. With practice, you no longer had to consciously tell your fingers what to do—they just knew—and you came to believe you were a good texter.

Your subconscious and self-image are closely linked. Your self-image determines your confidence toward a task. Your subconscious then works like a thermostat to try and keep your performance close to your self-image. When you're performing how you usually perform, everything's fine. But when you're performing better than usual, your subconscious kicks on like an air conditioner and tries to cool you off until you're back to your norm. When your performance goes cold, your subconscious turns up the heat to help you return to your norm. For good or bad, your subconscious will try to give you what you reliably do.

Take a golfer who usually shoots a score of 90 over eighteen holes. If he starts out really strong on a particular day—par, birdie, par, par—he'd be playing way better than his norm. What happens soon after? His subconscious air conditioner kicks on and tries to cool him off through overthinking or body hijacking.

Overthinking might sound like, "How do I keep this hot streak going?" or "Better not mess up on the next hole. It has a lot of water." Body hijacking occurs when his grip suddenly feels foreign or numb, and causes him to lose feel for his swing. The subconscious will try anything to get you back to your self-image comfort zone.

So how do you raise your subconscious thermostat to consistently play at a higher level without sabotaging yourself? There are two main solutions.

The first is to build a strong self-image for different areas of your game. The stronger your self-image, the less your subconscious will try to interfere. Here are a few strategies for strengthening your self-image:

- **Practice:** There's no substitute for physical practice. If you want to build a strong self-image, there must be evidence that you can do what you're setting out to do. If you're not willing to put in the work to build a strong self-image, you're leaving your performance to chance, which rarely works in your favor.

- **Positive affirmations:** Consistently repeat specific present tense phrases or commands that describe what you're doing or how you desire something to go. Repeat it to the point you believe it:

    I smash mistake pitches.

    I sink three-foot putts with ease.

    I swish shots late in games.

    I pitch low in the zone and let the ball sink naturally.

- **Mental movies:** Vividly visualize performing a task over and over as you'd like it to go until it's burned into your subconscious. A first-person perspective makes it more real and intimate.

- **Listen to your recall:** When you discuss your performances with others, do you talk about the negatives or positives? Your subconscious is always listening. If you emphasize the negatives to others, you're further ingraining the negatives.

- **Level of importance:** Whatever happens, ascribe a low level of importance to how you perform. Be intense about your process and preparation but be numb to your results. A low level of importance allows you to move on from mistakes and keep your emotions in check. Your subconscious feeds off emotional language. If you don't feed it emotions, it'll stay relatively quiet.

The second solution to raising your subconscious thermostat is to play in the present moment. Your subconscious takes what you've done in the past to predict how you'll perform. It also loves to project what pace you're on and insert itself if you're performing better or worse than normal. But when you demand your attention be in the now, you don't allow past performances or your current pace to impede the importance of doing what needs to be done now.

To summarize, you are the creator of your own self-image and thus have a large say over the information your subconscious feeds on. Choose to focus on images of winning and success. As your self-image starts to grow, you'll no longer be content with being part of the team. You'll expect yourself to become a major contributor.

This new self-image will require constant upkeep until it truly becomes who you are. Sure, the fear will still be there at times, but when you're willing to push past the discomfort, your subconscious will begin to believe you're as good as you say you are—and stay out of your way.

Do you dare believe you can win and win a lot? Do you dare put in the physical and mental work that success demands?

I have every confidence you will.

INNER ARROGANCE

A large part of having a grand vision is having what I call "inner arrogance." No one has to know how confident you are, but a certain amount of swagger needs to be there. You have to like your game more than anyone else's, even when others are more talented. You have to believe in your B game as much as your A game because you'll play from your B game much more often than your A game.

Baseball manager Leo Durocher once said of hard-nosed infielder Eddie "The Brat" Stanky back in the 1950s, "He can't hit, can't run, can't field. He just knows how to beat you." That's inner arrogance. Maximizing less to get the job done. You have it within you to show up every day with the best version of yourself and bring the challenge to others. It's your responsibility to make everyone else uncomfortable and get them off their game before they do it to you. It starts with envisioning yourself performing at your best until you believe it and do it.

You don't honestly know what you're capable of until you play with inner arrogance. Take ownership of the vision you have for yourself. Be unashamed about it. Pursue it. Ooze it.

You just might get everything you want.

So dare to believe.

Every. Single. Play.

BELIEVING PILLAR SUMMARY: YOUR FIVE KEYS TO CONFIDENCE

- **Perspective.** Believe you're the best athlete to get the job done at this moment, no matter how you've played.

- **Identity.** If you plan to get where you want to go, decide who you are, why you *really* play, and how you'll navigate the pleasures and pressures ready to detour your career.

- **Self-Compassion.** Failure will cause you to be your biggest critic, but with self-compassion, you become your best coach through mindfulness, common humanity, and self-kindness.

- **Vocabulary of Victory.** There's constant conflict waging between your ears, but a vocabulary of victory guarantees winning the war within.

- **Vision.** Your mind is happy to turn toward Negative Town, but when you consistently imagine the future you desire—whether it's the next play or the next thirty years—you give yourself concrete evidence to strive toward.

Pillar 2
BREATHING

14

EMOTIONS: A GAUGE, NOT A GUIDE

Jared earned a scholarship to play baseball at a Division 1 school by his junior year of high school. In his senior year, scouts considered him a prospect to watch for the MLB draft. I met Jared around that time, and he shared the pressure he felt from himself and others. In our Zoom calls, it was easy to see that he wasn't just tired—he was emotionally exhausted. Baseball used to be a joy. Now it felt like a stressful job to him.

Every at-bat became a life-or-death experience. If Jared succeeded, he felt one step closer to his Major League dreams. But when he struck out, particularly with runners on base, it was one step closer to the end of his career. At least in his eyes.

Jared fully understood baseball is a game of failure. Yet the emotional pull from failure and unrealistic expectations became overwhelming to the point where he was beating himself up before opponents got their chance at him.

In our first session, I explained to Jared that emotions are not a bad thing; they're just *a* thing. Emotions let him know how much the game means to him.

I made sure he understood that it was up to him how much meaning he gave any particular situation. Did two strikeouts *really* mean he was a terrible player? No. But the embarrassment and frustration he felt convinced himself otherwise. Emotions are tricky. The more intensely you feel them, the more believable they become.

But emotions are never meant to be a guide—only a gauge. Whether you use them as a gauge or a guide heavily dictates how you perform. Jared was allowing his anger and frustration to guide his performance, which primarily led to poor results and self-hatred. My goal was to help Jared use his emotions to gauge how he felt so he could then choose the right response to get back to playing to his potential.

EMOTIONS: A GAUGE, NOT A GUIDE

Emotional accountability means taking responsibility for how you think, feel, speak, and act. It takes persistent effort to manage your emotions. But there's freedom in self-control. There's never freedom in letting your emotions control you.

EMOTIONS AS A GUIDE

No matter how heavy emotions feel at times, they're like weather patterns—they come and go. The sun eventually shines even after the darkest storms. But in those dark moments, it's easier to remain in the dumps than pull yourself together. It's understandable. We're human, not robots. But while it's easy to be a slave to emotions in the moment, it's never the easier path long term.

Rarely will you *feel* like doing what needs to be done to get where you want to go in your sport. If you don't feel like waking up early for the gym—you won't. It's easier to sleep in. If you don't feel like pausing to take a breath after a questionable call—you won't. It's easier to let anger boil over to the next play. Those who are guided by emotions always fall behind the athletes who take the right action *despite* how they feel.

EMOTIONS AS A GAUGE

When you use your emotions to gauge how you're feeling, you stop over-identifying with that emotion. Instead, you learn to hold each emotion at arm's distance, like taking a picture in selfie mode and noticing how you're feeling at one particular moment in time. Consider this equation:

Emotional maturity = right emotion + proper
intensity + appropriate length of time

To help Jared build his emotional accountability, I gave him three questions to consider when feeling emotionally out of control:

- **Am I right to feel what I'm feeling?** Sports are highly emotional. The stronger you feel something, the more right you think you are to feel that way. While emotions are real, what you feel can still be different than what is true.

  When you're highly charged, pause and consider if you're right to feel the way you're feeling. Should a missed shot, an error, someone else getting the praise, or a strikeout cause you to lose it? Not if you're striving for emotional maturity.

  Sure, there are times when it's appropriate to be angry, sad, or frustrated. Being wronged on a bad call or muffing a routine play never feels good. But allowing feelings to overtake you during your performance or long after it won't help your situation. Instead, ask yourself what's the best way to feel right now to help you succeed and move forward. When you change your focus, you change your feelings. Is it easy? Not at first. But it does get easier.

- **Is this the right intensity for the situation?** Emotions can overwhelm or underwhelm you based on how much something means to you. The more meaning you give something, the greater the intensity.

  Does one questionable call or failure cause you to flip out? If it does, your emotional intensity is too high. If your team has lost five straight games and you don't care, your emotional intensity is too low. (This is often known as burnout.)

Your goal is to feel the proper intensity for the situation. Are you caring too much? Not enough? Or just right? Just right indicates you feel something enough to spark action to get better rather than stay bitter.

♦ **How long should I allow myself to feel this way?** It's okay *not* to be okay. It's just not ideal to stay there. Lingering emotions tend to fester until they turn from a gauge to a guide. Decide an appropriate amount of time to sit with whatever you're feeling. Then stand up and start doing what needs to be done, despite how you feel.

Action cures emotions. If it currently takes you a week to get over a bad call or bad game, work to cut that down to a few days. Then an evening. Then before you leave the field. When you can consistently move on from adversity by the next play, you approach emotional mastery.

It takes awareness to even ask yourself these questions. But knowing the right emotion to feel with the right intensity at the right time will always put you in the best position to play well. Be patient with yourself as you unlearn old habits and relearn new ones. Your emotions have the power to push you to pursue your dreams or persuade you to end them. It's your responsibility to change your feelings to be in harmony with what you want to achieve. This Breathing Pillar will teach you how.

First, it's important to understand how your emotions work so you can know what to do when they're trying to hijack your performance.

THREE EMOTION REGULATION SYSTEMS

Your mind and body always want to be comfortable. Sports try to make you as uncomfortable as possible. Your ability to manage—or regulate—your emotions is crucial to consistent high-level performance. In Paul Gilbert and Choden's book, *Mindful Compassion*, they touch on three emotion regulation systems: threat, drive, and soothe. When called upon, each system tries to meet the demands of the situation to help you return to a comfortable state.

Let's take a closer look at each one:

THREAT SYSTEM

Your threat system's main objective is to keep you alive. Intellectually, you grasp that sports aren't literally life or death. But emotionally, each failure can feel like a threat to the future of your athletic career (death). When you make a mistake, your body experiences stress. Stress triggers your threat system to pump adrenaline and cortisol through your body to prepare you to fight or flee the situation creating the discomfort.

Emotions like anxiety, anger, embarrassment, jealousy, and disgust (after failing) are associated with your threat system. They may seem like negative emotions, but they're not. These emotions act like security systems and trigger when you perceive a threat—like to your career goals. That's why they turn on automatically and fuel certain actions.

Here are some of the top threat system emotions and how to disarm them so you can train yourself to be comfortable when you're uncomfortable:

* **Anxiety.** Anxiety occurs when you're afraid of what might happen. Anxiety gives you tunnel vision for all that can go wrong:

  Don't make a mistake.

  Don't throw an interception.

  Don't give up a home run.

  These thoughts cause you to play timidly. Also, if you've ever felt the game speed up on you, anxiety is to blame. When you have a sleepless night ruminating over mistakes, that's anxiety trying to help you figure out how you messed up so you can keep your career alive tomorrow. The problem is anxiety is only good at amplifying the problems rather than finding the solutions. Thus, you're left with even greater stress.

- **Disarming anxiety:** The quicker you want out of anxiety, the slower you need to take each moment. When anxious, breathing is more important than believing because an anxious mind is an unclear mind.

  Breathing allows you to ease the threat level and regain a proper perspective of what is true. The deep breath combined with mindfulness of the moment reminds you to be where your feet are and that you're the right person for the situation. Then you can focus on what you need to do rather than what you're trying to avoid. *Don't let this goal score* becomes *Get big and move your feet to block the ball.* Breathing and telling yourself what to do are in your control and give you the best chance of getting out of a jam with minimal damage.

- **Anger.** While anxiety makes you want to flee, anger prepares you to fight. Anger floods you with focus and energy to help you play aggressively. What you focus that energy on will make or break you. Athletes and coaches who use anger as a guide rather than a gauge end up apologizing for kicking a Gatorade jug, smashing an iPad (or two), breaking a hand after punching a wall, or uttering words they can't take back. What anger will drive you to do may feel right at the time, but it's rarely the right move. It's easy to let anger have its way. But it's worth it to manage the rage you're feeling.

  When used as a gauge, anger informs you of what something means to you. If you've been practicing a particular aspect of your sport and it doesn't get rewarded during competition, you have a right to be angry or frustrated. But be careful, anger leads to aggression, and aggression leads to action before seeing a play develop. For instance, throwing interceptions and taking bad swings are good examples of forcing action before seeing action. Anger also leads to tension, and tension slows your muscles.

- **Disarming anger:** Breathing, mindfulness, and common human-ity are three anger extinguishers. Breathing calms you down, and mindfulness helps you name and reframe your anger as some-thing you're experiencing rather than something overtaking you. Common humanity can help you see that what you're angry about, like a referee call, doesn't just happen to you, it happens to many others. Once you are back under control, ask if whatever's got you angry was worth being angry about. It's usually not.

- **Embarrassment.** Embarrassment is worrying about what others think when you perform worse than expected. Embarrassment is a fleeing emotion that wants you to escape the discomfort of judgment, and it tries to shame you into playing better so you can remain accepted by your peers.

- **Disarming embarrassment:** Deep breaths, common humanity, and self-kindness are paramount to disarming embarrassment. Errors, mistakes, failures, and bad moments happen to everyone and almost everyone wants to beat themself up over mistakes. Self-kindness will combat embarrassment with words of encouragement and wisdom that gives you the freedom to make errors and look foolish at times, because it's going to happen anyway.

  When appropriate, combat embarrassment with humor. You'll be amazed at what laughing something off can do for your rebound rate. Don't wait until the end of your career to look back and say, "I wish I didn't care so much what people thought of me." When you adopt that thinking now, you'll notice a significant drop in how often you get embarrassed. The people who love you now will still love you no matter how you play.

- **Disgust.** Disgust is less about what others think and more about your opinion of yourself. When appropriately used as a gauge, disgust reveals that you believe in yourself and know you can do better. Feelings of disgust keep you from going through the motions and will whip your focus into shape to start performing how you know you can. If you don't experience some level of disgust, it's because you don't believe you should be performing better than you are.

While disgust's intentions are good, its methods aren't. Disgust tries to motivate you by beating you up while you're down. You don't need another self-inflicted verbal or physical beating after messing up. If poor play continues, disgust can turn into self-hatred and a loss of love for your sport.

- **Disarming disgust:** Breathing and self-kindness are two ways to combat disgust. Self-kindness reminds you how good you are even when you just messed up. Self-kindness uses soothing touch to heal the internal disconnect. Place your hand on your heart or somewhere comfortable to feel the warmth and connection needed to mend. During adversity, you need yourself more than ever. Show up without judgment. Only kindness.

- **Jealousy.** Jealousy is feeling threatened by what someone has or what you feel you lack, like talent, skills, athleticism, looks, or a scholarship. The absence of those attributes make you feel inferior and sets off your threat system. If someone can jump higher, throw harder, or run faster than you, he or she stands in your way from playing at the next level. If someone gets a scholarship before you, that's one less spot at the next level. Jealousy can fuel you to fight or flee. When you feel inferior, your focus is on everything they have instead of what you bring to the table. Advantage them.

- **Disarming jealousy:** Take deep breaths and think about your common humanity. Nobody is perfect and everybody to some degree wishes they had what others have. A great antidote to jealousy is thankfulness and admiration. Thankfulness does its best to remember how talented, skilled, and unique you are. Jealousy does it's best to forget those qualities.

    Admiration puts a positive spin on jealousy by looking at others' strengths as something to aspire to rather than fear. Admiration fosters togetherness. Jealousy causes division. Instead of feeling threatened or jealous of good competition, choose to be thankful that you have a chance to play against the best. Doing so will bring out your best if you're prepared. Is there a chance you will fail? Sure. But your competition is human, too, with their own set of insecurities and shortcomings.

- **Pain.** Pain is the most automatic alarm set off by your threat system. Pain lets you know right away where you're injured or what muscles are working hard during workouts. Your threat system immediately goes to work on healing what's hurting. All your body wants to do is heal.

  Injury pain tells you you're hurt and need to stop. Workout pain does the same, but you know this is a time to keep going. Your body only wants to be comfortable, so it's your responsibility to know the difference between injury pain and the pain of hard work where you need to push through.

- **Disarming pain:** Breathing and self-compassion in general. You don't want to disarm injury pain with Advil or other anti-inflammatory drugs. Listen to your body and get the proper care. Mentally, mindfulness helps you breathe and keep your injury in perspective that it's a setback, and not the end, in most cases. Common humanity reminds you that injuries happen to every athlete. Self-kindness helps you comfort yourself when your mind wants to freak out and even beat yourself up for getting injured.

  For workout pain that's persuading you to slow down or stop, self-compassion works too. Mindfulness helps you realize the pain you're feeling is temporary and necessary for getting where you want to go. Common humanity reminds you that every athlete striving to become elite has to endure the same pain.

  When you're slowing down or stopping your workout, self-kindness can activate the fierce side of you that motivates you to keep going because it's in your best interest in light of your long term goals. You're not in danger. You're just uncomfortable.

Take your mind off of pain by singing a song. Build yourself up with your vocabulary of victory. Workout pain reaches a threshold and then can't get any worse. Do your best to embrace the pain rather than resist it. When you do, it makes your workouts a little more enjoyable.

Your threat system is extremely valuable when used as a gauge rather than a guide. When used as a gauge, emotions like anger, anxiety, embarrassment, and jealousy become helpers in alerting you to potential career killers. Acknowledge what you're feeling and decide how you want to channel the energy and focus that emotion provides. What you focus that energy on will make or break you.

DRIVE SYSTEM

Your drive system motivates you to pursue and attain your goals. The drive within you urges you to go to the gym and rewards you with endorphins and dopamine afterward. Joy, happiness, and excitement are associated with your drive system. Similar to your threat system, the jolt your drive system receives can elevate your heart rate and get your thoughts racing, but in anticipation of experiencing good moments rather than dreading something terrible.

Without your drive system, you'd never strive to achieve greatness or care to make anything of yourself. It's necessary to tap into this system if you plan to become an elite athlete. But like anything, too much is too much. The constant chase of the good feelings associated with winning, padding stats sheets, and basking in the adoration of others can become addicting to the point where you experience great frustration or depression if you don't meet the high standards you set for yourself.

A negative side effect of an unbalanced drive system is increased pressure to prove yourself and avoid embarrassment. Ironically, a hyperactive drive system can activate what I call your drive/threat system, where something worth looking forward to turns into something you dread.

Athletes understand they have a small window to compete at a high level and, hopefully, get paid to compete one day. Some athletes with an out-of-control drive system are willing to risk their bodies and careers by taking performance-enhancing drugs to get ahead, catch up, or maintain their level of play. Former Major League Baseball player Alex Rodriguez said he took steroids after signing with the Texas Rangers in 2001 because he felt the pressure to live up to the biggest sports contract ever at the time. Being linked to performance-enhancing drugs cost him his reputation, a season-long suspension late in his career, and likely, a place in the Baseball Hall of Fame.

Other athletes feel the need to unwind with alcohol or drugs to get a quick fix of dopamine to feel good. This happened to Josh Hamilton, who you read about earlier. Addiction to feeling good or numbing the pain lost him the best years of his career. Every athlete comes from different circumstances that drive them to do what they do. Don't let an overly ambitious drive system urge you to risk your reputation, health, and future on the slight chance you make it big.

That said, your drive system is crucial to pursuing your dreams, but when out of balance, it'll get you to believe the work you put in is never enough, leaving you unable to find contentment. That's where your soothe system comes to the rescue.

SOOTHE SYSTEM

Your soothe system may be your most important yet least utilized system. As a competitor, your threat system is worried about whether you're good enough, and your drive system is constantly telling you that you're not doing enough.

But your soothe system carries the ability to pump the breaks and calm you down. One of your soothe system's superpowers is contentment.

Contentment allows you to be satisfied and at peace with how things are—not needing anything or feeling the need to do more. Athletes who neglect their soothe system will never be satisfied. They rarely think they're good enough or have done enough.

Unlike the other two systems, your soothe system isn't on autopilot. You are responsible for activating it, which can prove challenging. Constant stimulation from phones, social media, TV, and needing to be around friends also makes it hard to quiet the mind and body to find the rest and contentment you need. In the next chapter, you'll learn how to activate your soothe system to combat overactive threat and drive systems.

But first, Gilbert and Choden, in *Mindful Compassion*, provide an activity using three circles to help you apply everything you just learned about your emotion regulation systems. I have modified it slightly by adding a fourth circle. Have fun with the exercise and approach it with curiosity rather than criticism.

THE FOUR CIRCLES EXERCISE

On a piece of paper, [or scan the QR code in the opening pages to download the worksheet] spread out the words *threat, drive, drive/threat,* and *soothe*. Then, draw a circle proportionate to the amount of time you operate from each system.

How much mental energy do you spend being afraid, angry, disgusted, or embarrassed? Draw a circle proportionate to the number of triggers that set off your threat system. Are you triggered by being late to practice? Making mistakes? Missing shots? Drawing comparisons? Hearing rumors? Write out each trigger. These are your energy sappers.

What in your sport excites you or brings you joy? What gets you out of bed? Draw a circle proportionate to the mental energy you gain thinking about your dreams and seeing your hard work pay off, which triggers your drive system. Write down what creates a positive feeling about your sport. These are your energizers.

What in your sport should be fun but leaves you fearful? For example, hitting is one of the best parts of baseball. But the baseball player who's worried about striking out or what others think will be driven by the fear of failing rather than the fun of possibly succeeding. Draw a circle around *threat/drive system* that represents the amount of mental space this mindset takes up and list each trigger. These are energy sappers that should be energizers.

Finally, what helps you slow down, relax, and be content? Contentment is being okay with what is. Draw a circle around the things you like to do, places that bring you peace, hobbies you get lost in, and the loving people who trigger your *soothe system*. These are your refreshers.

After this activity, discover where you're spending most of your mental energy. How are your emotions sapping, energizing, or refreshing you? What circle would you like to see grow? What circle would you like to see shrink?

Many athletes discover they spend too much time in the *threat, drive,* or *threat/drive* circles and neglect their *soothe* circle. No system is necessarily good or bad. Each one has its value.

Determine the ideal amount of time you'd like to spend in each circle to get the most out of you. Since the *soothe system* is often the most underdeveloped system, we'll now spend time learning how to build it up.

15

BREATHING

When we start paying attention to the breath . . . breathing is no longer just breathing. It is our centering point. Our focusing anchor.

—John Kabat-Zinn, founder of the Stress Reduction Clinic

Most athletes agree that being relaxed is their ideal performance state. Even in sports like football, where getting jacked up is part of the culture, relaxed and calm can still be king. Deep breathing is your key to calm and relaxed play. When you bring awareness to each breath, you invite yourself into the present moment where action is happening. Here are some different breathing styles and exercises to activate your soothe system for greater focus, calmness, confidence and clarity.

FORMAL BREATHING

Formal breathing is where you set aside time to be with your breath in the present moment. You can do this by lying down, sitting up, relaxing in nature, or getting quiet on the inside in the locker room prior to a game. Deep breaths allow you to remain peaceful when everything around you is chaotic. The deep breath builds your awareness. The greater your awareness, the better you can see the game clearly.

Since there are crowd noise and distractions when you play, don't worry about finding a quiet place to do your breathing exercises. During the 2022 college football season, the University of Michigan quarterback, J.J. McCarthy, made time before games to do breathing exercises while sitting on the sideline. With his eyes closed and noise-canceling headphones on, he took time to get quiet and be present with every deep breath.

Between rounds of the 2022 Home Run Derby, the defending champion, Pete Alonso of the New York Mets, was captured on video in the batting cage area underneath Dodger Stadium, sitting on a table doing breathing exercises and visualizing.

Why do these great athletes do breathing exercises? Because of the "need to focus where our feet are," Pete Alonso was quoted as saying.

ACTIVE BREATHING

Active breathing is much less planned than formal breathing and can be done throughout your day. The goal remains to be mindful of each breath in the moment. You can practice active breathing while walking to class, feeling your feet contact the ground or doing dishes, feeling the brush move across each plate. The point is to pay attention to what you're experiencing in the moment.

The late sports psychology guru, Ken Ravizza, used to say, "When you're putting on your batting gloves . . . put on your batting gloves. When you're grabbing your bat . . . grab you're your bat. Be where your feet are. Be here now."

Active breathing helps you build an awareness of what's happening right now. Formal and active breathing complement each other: the better you get at one, the better you get at the other. See which type of breathing is more effective for you, but work to develop both.

AWARENESS BREATHING

I challenge you to begin viewing breathing as much more than air going in and out of your lungs, keeping you alive. Treat breathing as it truly is, the most convenient and effective tool for building awareness of your thoughts and feelings. When you're aware, you're awake. The rhythms of your heart and breath work together to inform you of changes to your mental and physical state.

How might games go differently if you take a moment to pause and check in with yourself? Your performance can spin out of control when your heart and mind start racing without you even being aware it's happening. If you don't realize when you're losing control, how will you know to take a deep breath to slow down and regain composure?

BREATHING EXERCISE: SITTING AWARENESS

Awareness starts by literally sitting with your breath. Sit somewhere comfortably and begin to breathe in through your nose and out of your mouth. Bring your awareness to the inhale as your chest and belly rise and then to the exhale as your chest and belly fall.

As you increase your ability to pay attention to the breath, you build your capacity to effectively focus on one thing among many distractions. Don't try to control your breath. Just be with it. Be fascinated with it. The more attracted you are to your breath, the less distracted your mind will be to anything else.

SPORT APPLICATION: R.A.I.N.N.

The acronym R.A.I.N.N. stands for *recognize, allow, investigate, not identify with,* and *nurture.* Many athletes try to outplay their emotions, run from them, or deny them. None of these are effective long-term strategies. Mindfully turning toward your emotions, as scary as that prospect sounds for some, is always the quickest road back to peak performance. Practice visualizing situations you currently struggle with and use R.A.I.N.N. to help diffuse them. With practice, you can begin to implement the acronym into your performance.

Recognize: We often experience an emotion without even realizing it. Your challenge is to recognize what's going on inside of you while it's happening without judging yourself for having that emotion. Sometimes your legs will shake during pregame introductions, or your heart will feel like it's in your throat when you step up to the free throw line, down by one point with seconds to play. Recognize that it's happening and name it. *Oh, this is nervousness I'm feeling,* you think as you bounce the ball. When you name the emotion you're feeling, it's easier to be present with it rather than deny it, run from it, or over-identify with it.

Allow: Can you allow yourself to be present with this emotion right now? Remember, emotions are there one minute or a few seconds and are gone the next. As you recognize emotions when they arise and allow them space to breathe, you're showing the emotion that you're the one in control. This causes the emotion lose its power, and it usually leaves on its own. Sometimes you're one play away from being mentally balanced again.

When you can't afford to experience certain emotions in the moment, you can resist them for a time to do what needs to be done. You've trained for the moment you're in. Embody the emotion you need for it.

Investigate: Once you've recognized and allowed an emotion to be there, it's time to investigate how this emotion influences your thoughts, feelings, and body in real time with a curious eye rather than a critical eye. That way, when it happens in a game, you're not so surprised that you amplify the emotion.

Not identify with: Emotions are always present but never permanent. This should be an encouraging reminder to help you return to emotional stability. Your ability to separate yourself from any emotion by thinking, *I notice [insert emotion] is currently present within me, but I know I am not this emotion, and it's not permanent.* This confirms you hold the power.

Nuture: When you're able to recognize, allow, and investigate your emotions without directly identifying with them, you become available to nurture yourself with what you need to get through and get back to playing well. Think of a baby in distress. A compassionate mother doesn't scold a baby for feeling what he's feeling. She holds her baby son close and hushes him sweetly. The typical result? The baby is comforted and calms down.

As you begin to be that comforting presence in your life to ease your threat or drive systems, you'll be able to handle stressful moments effectively when your emotions want to run rampant. Your job isn't to fix how you feel. You're feeling that way for a reason. Your goal is to acknowledge your feelings and be supportive until you regain composure for the next moment.

FOCUS BREATHING

Every athlete struggles with focus. Some believe concentrating really hard on their task for long periods is the key to being focused, but it's not. Straining to concentrate works against you as it burns too much mental energy and leads to mental mistakes. Instead, know what's important in the moment and allow it to grab *your* attention. When you desire something, you don't have to work hard to give it your full attention. But alas, we are human, and distractions will inevitably find us.

Your breath is a lifelong partner you can always rely on as a focus tool. The most important moment is always right now. A focused awareness on breathing helps you to be here for it and calls you back when your mind wanders.

BREATHING EXERCISE: EYES ON THE PRIZE

Start with deep belly breaths for a minute. Then, take your awareness to the most critical thing in your sport: the ball (or puck, etc.). Picture it in your mind. Let it turn if it wants. See the details. You might notice how your mind fills in the blank space, like adding a backdrop stadium or gym. Allow that to happen. But keep your focus on that object. When you feel your mind drifting, raise your hand until you can gently bring your attention back to the object of your desire. This will strengthen your focus ability.

SPORT APPLICATION: ENERGY STOPLIGHT

Where your focus goes, your energy flows. It's your responsibility to direct your focus to what's most important. The energy stoplight comprises green, gray, yellow, and red lights and serves as an awareness strategy to help you redirect your focus and energy to what's essential.

Green means go. You're focused on what's important and feel you can dominate the moment as you confidently tell yourself what to do. What situations cause you to be in green? What do you feel? What do you tell yourself?

Gray means neutral. You're focused on the facts of the situation and on what you need to do despite how you feel. You see the situation as it truly is—not better or worse. Neutrality is always available. When in neutral, what do you feel and say?

Yellow means you're starting to tilt. You're distracted by what's going wrong and are beginning to be guided by doubt, anger, or fear. You're telling yourself what *not* to do. What situations cause you to be in yellow? What do you feel? What do you tell yourself?

Red means full tilt. You're amplifying everything that's gone wrong and allowing emotions like anger, bitterness, and revenge to guide your mind and body. What situations cause you to be in red? What do you feel? What do you tell yourself?

Writing out your situational triggers is key to seeing how they influence your thoughts and feelings. Right now, one play can take you from green to yellow or red. But when you work on this exercise, at some point it'll take two or three poor plays before you leave green. Then, eventually, an entire game. Work on your energy stoplight off the field, like when you're in a traffic jam or taking a test. It'll help you improve on checking what color you're in.

Most athletes go their entire careers without tapping into the power of their breath. Instead, they allow their emotions to kill their confidence. But as you grow to rely on your breath as your greatest ally, your threat system doesn't have to destroy your performance. This powerful ally lives right under your nose and is only a deep breath away.

YOUR EMOTIONAL IMPACT ON OTHERS

While it's up to everyone to control their emotions, you can still impact how others feel. Consider the different dynamics of a locker room: backgrounds, personalities, goals, motivations, and playing status. There's going to be conflict within your team. What role you play is up to you.

NEGATIVE EMOTIONAL IMPACT ON OTHERS

Everyone has heard of the term "bad apple" to reference a teammate whose behavior has a detrimental influence on the team. This is the emotional impact a single individual can have on those around her. "Bad apples" do it in any number of ways.

One common problem among teams is the narcissist who's always looking out for No. 1. They place the blame on others and never consider themselves to be the problem. Hall of Fame baseball player Reggie Jackson, known as one of sports' most infamous narcissists, said, "Sometimes I underestimate the magnitude of me." Jackson also said he was the "straw that stirs the drink."

These types don't necessarily try to be leaders. They often isolate themselves because they're so preoccupied with themselves. Even when they think they're not calling attention to themselves, no one's fooled. The tension is real.

Another common problem is the team leader who isn't cut out to be one. This person is quick to publicly put others on blast with no regard for their feelings. These leaders get ignored or laughed at behind their backs. Good teams largely play below their potential due to these so-called leaders and their emotional abuse. Don't be this type of leader, and don't allow these types to ruin your performance or love for your sport.

Another way you impact teammates emotionally is through your attitude. What's going on internally will win out externally. This could be a bad attitude that manifests itself in poor body language. Jealousy turns into bitter trash talk. Anger leads to tension and confrontation. And anxiety leads to avoidance. These emotions cause breakdown and division within a team.

If you let emotions be your guide, your words and actions will add to the frustrations that already exist. Let your emotions be a gauge of how you feel, and deal with them appropriately by either addressing an issue directly with a person or ask for help from someone you can trust. That way, you can be part of the solution rather than the problem.

POSITIVE EMOTIONAL IMPACT ON OTHERS

In Joan Ryan's book, *Intangibles*, she describes Major League Baseball player Jonny Gomes, who played fourteen seasons, as a super-carrier—someone with an uncanny ability to help teams win. Gomes helped bring winning baseball to notoriously bad teams. He came up with Tampa Bay Rays in 2003, who hadn't had a winning season in its relatively short existence. By 2008, Gomes helped them get to the World Series. He assisted the Cincinnati Reds in erasing a fifteen-year playoff drought in 2010. In 2012, the outfielder was a catalyst on an Oakland A's team that was predicted to lose 100 games. Instead, their record was 94-68, good enough to make the playoffs. He won a World Series with the Boston Red Sox in 2013 and the Kansas City Royals in 2015.

Jonny Gomes wasn't a superstar. By the numbers, he wasn't even that good of a player. No one could quantify the chemistry he kindled in the clubhouse, yet everyone felt it. He had a knack for turning teams into families. Joan Ryan describes Gomes's personality and presence through the eyes of Gomes's former teammate and pitcher, Brandon McCarthy. McCarthy recalls meeting Gomes for the first time in an off-season workout facility when they were both young major leaguers. Ryan writes:

> McCarthy kept a low profile, as would be expected of a newbie. But Gomes dove right in, ragging on guys, telling jokes. McCarthy had never seen anyone like him. He changed the vibe of the workout group as soon as he blew through the door every morning. "He had a kind of power over everyone," McCarthy told me.

What was Jonny Gomes's secret sauce? Ryan's answer: "Gomes seemed to smell what guys needed. He knew when to joke, inspire, push, and teach. He found ways to nurture their confidence." Gomes's heart was set on the needs of others. He was secure with himself and his role on the team, which allowed him to enjoy the success of others.

Teammates described him as unselfish and an open book in sharing his knowledge and tips that could lead to gaining an edge—an uncommon practice at the highest level. His attitude and approach were known to rub off on teammates. Soon enough, he had twenty-five guys fighting *for* each other, not with each other.

Many failures and mess-ups that divide teams get washed away when teammates strive together as one unit. Jonny poured into his teammates until they believed in themselves. You can do the same. When you get your eyes off your problems and start building up your teammates, you'll become your version of Jonny Gomes. As you lead with love, humor, and trust, teammates will feel it and hopefully catch on.

OTHERS' EMOTIONAL IMPACT ON YOU

The words and actions of others can definitely hurt. Especially when coming from a teammate, coach, or parent. But according to author Marshall B. Rosenberg in *Nonviolent Communication*, what others say and do may be the stimulus, but never the cause of your feelings. No one can make you feel anything. According to Rosenberg, there are four ways to receive a negative comment or action:

1. **Blame yourself.** Teammates and captains can quickly blame you between plays for making mistakes. Criticism taken personally often leads to self-criticism in the form of guilt, shame, frustration, or embarrassment. These emotions steal your confidence and persuade you to play timidly. Your motivation becomes *not* to mess up rather than to play to win with joy and enthusiasm.

2. **Blame others.** A referee's call can be upsetting, but it doesn't have to upset you. When you blame others for your failures, anger ensues and leads to overaggressive play and unforced errors.

3. **Sense your feelings and needs.** When you're on the wrong end of a call on the field, you have the opportunity to pause and check in. For baseball or softball players, when a pitch is called a strike that was clearly a ball, they could pause and internally say, *I feel frustrated because I pride myself on laying off balls out of the strike zone.* By turning attention toward the feeling (frustration), the batters maintain emotional control and realize their frustration stems not from the umpire call itself, but from their desire to be rewarded for having a good eye at the plate.

4. **Sense others' feelings and needs.** Even amid negativity, you can still pause to consider the root of words or actions toward you. This is how you find compassion for others and keep your performance on track.

When you pause to consider a teammate's feelings and needs, you might realize the reason she's yelling at you is because she's scared that if you don't play well, your team will lose. If you lose, college coaches won't watch your team. And she will miss out on earning a scholarship. So, she yells at you to get you to play better.

Similarly, pausing to remember umpires are human beings prone to making mistakes will help you understand why they sometimes make bad calls. Umpires don't want to be the focus. They want to call a fair game to the best of their ability. When you have compassion toward the officials, it helps you remain even-keeled and under control.

What others say or do will still sting, but it doesn't have to knock you off your game emotionally. When you accept responsibility for your feelings by fully understanding your needs, you'll blame others less and be bothered less when negative words and actions are directed at you.

EMOTIONS FLOW WHERE EXPECTATIONS GO

I was enjoying time with my daughter at an indoor trampoline park when we went over to the basketball area. While playing H-O-R-S-E, I sunk a shot from about fifteen feet away with a squishy ball. It was her turn to make the same shot.

She said, "Oh, I won't make this," and her body language immediately slumped. She allowed her expectations to dictate her emotions. Her emotions then sent a message to her body about how to perform.

Countless athletes kill their performance due to their belief about what might happen. Newsflash: you don't know what the future holds. And your past doesn't have to predict your future. In *The Last Dance*, a documentary about Michael Jordan and the 1997-1998 Bulls, a scene in one of the episodes captures a friendly shootout during practice between Jordan and some teammates. They were shooting from the sideline near half-court when Jordan's turn came up. The cameras panned to him, and a teammate asked, "Mike, you nervous?"

Jordan grabbed a basketball, bounced it a few times, eyed the basket, and said, "Why would I worry about a shot I haven't taken yet?" Then, he swished the shot from near half-court and slinked away laughing. Jordan didn't let worry add pressure to his performance. He didn't allow something that hadn't happened yet to infiltrate his thinking. He focused on making the shot. Not missing it.

Pressure comes from expectations. The word *expectation* refers to an anticipated future outcome. We have strong ties to the things we want in performance. High expectations that fall short make you sick with disappointment, but expectations that are fulfilled are met with exhilaration. Since failure is so much more prevalent than success, it's vital to put expectations in the right place. Or not have them at all.

If you want to experience less pressure and disappointment, drop your expectations. It doesn't mean you don't care. It means you're more interested in the present moment than what might happen in the future.

How often do you let lofty expectations disrupt your ability to play in the moment? How often do you waste energy overthinking situations that rarely come to pass the way you magnify them in your mind? Worry focuses on the worst possible outcome. When your body listens to you worrying—and it's always listening—it plays right into your worst fears.

Tell yourself what you need to do rather than allow your mind to entertain all the things that could go wrong. Your performance depends on it. If you're going to have expectations, then expect to play as well as you've prepared.

FINAL THOUGHTS ON EMOTIONS

- ◆ You decide whether today will be a good or bad day despite what happens on the field or court.

- ◆ Your outlook determines your emotions.

- ◆ True sorrow isn't fixed with a smile, a drink, or a pint of ice cream.

- ◆ When the party's over, negative feelings will resurface, so be prepared to deal with them.

The most significant outcomes of emotional accountability will be the fortitude you'll have to handle every aspect of your sport and the freedom you'll feel to have fun playing. Plus, you'll be more enjoyable to be around, no matter how things are going.

Pillar 3
BODY

16

BODY

Your mind is your body, and your body is your mind.

—Jim Loehr, sports psychologist

You can have a Major League body, but if you have a Little League mind . . . you have a Little League body because the mind tells the body what to do. You cannot separate the mind and the body.

Before a big moment in a game, does your body ever shake uncontrollably? This may feel like a purely physical response, but it isn't. Shaking stems from a thought that gave life to an emotion that told your body how to feel. How you perceive a situation—either as a threat or a challenge—makes all the difference in how your body responds.

When you perceive a performance situation as a threat, your threat system prepares you to either fight (a form of anger), take flight (because of anxiety), or freeze (because you feel overwhelmed). But when you perceive a performance situation as a challenge, your drive system gets excited and readies you to compete.

Physically, your threat and drive systems can feel the same. For example, fear and excitement—two very different emotions—will each cause your heart rate to pick up and your mind to race. But mentally, fear and excitement are the equivalents of a gazelle being chased by a lion.

GAZELLE, LION, OR MOTHER BEAR?

During a chase, the lion and gazelle each have adrenaline coursing through their bodies, which allows them to run at top speeds. The lion is on the hunt and has its eyes on catching its prey. The gazelle knows it's being hunted and is focused on not getting caught. In sports, lion mode means you're solely focused on succeeding in the moment while gazelle mode means your mind is distracted by all the potential consequences of failing. What percentage of your performance are you in the mindset of the gazelle versus the lion?

Alex was a Division 1 softball player in her first Fall Ball season. She was struggling with her hitting. After explaining the difference between a gazelle and a lion to her, I asked her which animal she felt more like.

"Of late, I'd say I feel like the gazelle," she responded.

"Thanks for being honest," I replied. "My goal is to help you go from a gazelle to a lioness—and tap into the mother bear mode when necessary."

And then I proceeded to describe the differences to Alex.

GAZELLE MODE (THREAT SYSTEM)

Your threat system's number-one job is to keep you alive. In sports, not being good enough is your biggest threat. If you're not good enough, you're definitely not starting. If you're not starting, you're a bench player, which is one step closer to being out of your sport. At least that was what ran through Alex's mind as she ruminated about her hitting struggles. Each time she stepped to the plate, the fear of failing activated her gazelle mode, causing her to focus on not failing.

From a physiological standpoint, it wasn't all Alex's fault. During at-bats when she felt threatened, her body flooded with adrenaline and cortisol, the stress hormone, which naturally injects the mind with negative thinking—in particular—worst-case scenario thinking. Alex's prior success and any positive self-talk strategies didn't stand a chance against the direct cortisol injection of negativity, causing her to lose trust and confidence in herself.

When you believe you're under threat, here's what adrenaline and cortisol do to your body, why they do it, and how they tend to harm your performance:

- **You experience a high heart rate.** Adrenaline forces your heart to pump quicker, pushing oxygenated blood and glucose (sugar) in greater volume to your muscles.

  Why? The more oxygen and sugar you receive, the more energy you'll have to fight or flee.

  Harms: A racing heart leads to racing thoughts and rushed mechanics. Under stress, cortisol naturally causes you to think negatively. This is why stressful situations can cause you to doubt yourself and lose confidence. You often find yourself in *try mode* instead of *trust mode*.

- **You experience rapid breathing.** Under threat, your brain tells you to consume more air.

  Why? Your mind believes you'll need more oxygen for the situation.

  Harms: This can lead to hyperventilating and a feeling of being out of control and afraid for your life. Passing out is actually your body's way of keeping you alive.

- **You experience butterflies or nausea.** Cortisol arrives soon after adrenaline and shuts down stomach acids, enzymes, and blood flow to the organs not necessary for fighting or fleeing.

  Why? Your stomach isn't important at the moment, but your limbs are. Cortisol even shuts down insulin production in the kidneys, which causes your liver to produce glucose (sugar) for extra energy.

  Harms: This can cause distraction and discomfort and even the need to throw up.

- **You experience jitters, shaking, tension, or numbness.** Stressful situations can overstimulate your nervous system, producing simultaneous muscle contractions for quicker movements.

Why? Your nervous system readies itself to meet the demand with speed and power.

Harms: When your muscles are firing without your permission, your movements are more jagged rather than smooth. Tight grips are a common problem in tense moments. Muscle tension can also make you feel "heavy" or frozen, almost unable to move. Prolonged muscle tension fatigues the muscles, which leads to injuries.

◆ **Sweaty palms and face:** Your sympathetic nervous system opens the sweat glands of your hands, feet, face, and armpits.

Why? Sweating increases your ability to get away (slippery) and releases body odor, which activates the fear system in your opponents.

Harms: Sweat can get in your eyes to disrupt your view or cause your grip to be slick, hindering your confidence. Heavy sweat loss can result in dehydration, mental fatigue, cramps, and injury.

The gazelle mode is a necessary feature for keeping you alive. But in sports, where a life-and-death situation is rare, the gazelle mode loses its value and often hurts more than helps. Even when your emotions are persuading you to flee, fight the feeling and strive to become a lion on the field.

LION MODE (DRIVE SYSTEM)

We won't rehash the physical feelings involved with the lion mode since overall they are the same as the gazelle mode. Both modes supply adrenaline to prepare you to perform and tap into every resource you have. But when you choose to see situations as a challenge, your drive system injects you with dopamine, which motivates you to focus on the rewards of success rather than the consequences of failure. In lion mode, you can tap into a feeling of invincibility, not caring about anything other than getting the job done because you know you can.

When a lion is on the chase, it's not worried about anything chasing it. He knows he's in the power position. You can too.

Experiencing success or seeing improvement leads to more dopamine, which supplies greater motivation and confidence. As we already learned in the Breathing Pillar, your drive system can become hyperactive if success changes from a desired goal to a necessity. Necessity leads to unnecessary pressure. When this happens, you begin to work from your threat system rather than your drive system. You transform from a lion to a gazelle.

How can you stop this from happening? By going into the mother bear mode.

MOTHER BEAR MODE (SOOTHE SYSTEM)

When under duress from your threat system or an overly competitive drive system, it's time to manually activate your soothe system—or mother bear mode. According to author Kristin Neff in *Self-Compassion*, the hormone oxytocin is a natural bonding hormone that's released during social contact or from mother-infant bonding. Oxytocin reduces fear and anxiety while boosting feelings of trust, confidence, and contentment. Unlike cortisol and dopamine that release automatically, oxytocin can be released through physical touch, music, and exercise.

When a baby cries, she's crying out for help. When held close and whispered gently to by a parent, what's the result? The baby feels soothed, relaxed, calm, and confident, and she trusts she's safe again.

These are the same feelings you want for your body when performing: relaxation, calmness, the ability to trust your skills, and the confidence to go out and play the way you know how. Your job is to tap into your mother bear mode through gentle words and soothing touch to provide that calming effect for yourself. This can be the difference in rebounding or not.

In one of my sessions with Alex, I had her do fifty jumping jacks to trigger her threat system so she could simulate her typical stress responses of heavy breathing, a racing heart, and negative thoughts while hitting. Then I had her sit down and imagine walking to the plate with her chin up and chest out while using a four-breath-in-eight-breath-out breathing technique to initiate her soothe system. When she stepped into the batter's box, she repeated, "See the ball well and smash."

Then I asked her to place a hand on her heart. After about thirty seconds, I asked her what she felt. "Warmth and connection," she replied.

Stressful situations often cause us to feel numb with a kind of out-of-body disconnect. Yet through positive body language, breathing, physical touch, and gentle words, Alex was able to become her best support system by softening her threat system. It just takes remembering to do it when you're emotionally triggered.

Mother bear mode is much more than just a calming aid. A mother bear can protect her young (threat system), provide for her young (drive system), and nurture or play with her young (soothe system). In essence, the mother bear mode can be your one-stop shop to supply your body with whatever it needs to meet the demand.

If you choose to adopt this mindset, you have access to whatever you need to meet the challenges you face. It doesn't always mean you'll win. You just won't defeat yourself.

BODY LANGUAGE: CHANGING
FROM THE OUTSIDE IN

Your body communicates on the outside what you're feeling on the inside. When you're unable to find confidence from within, you'll need to reverse the process and work from the outside in. No matter what mood you're in right now, if you smile for thirty seconds, there's no way you can stay in a bad mood. When you lack confidence, put your hands on your hips and puff out your chest like Superman for one minute. Then try to feel weak and afraid. You can't.

Your body language speaks loud and clear. It will help or hurt you depending on how you use it. It's easy to look confident when you're feeling confident. But after messing up, your anger, frustration, or embarrassment will show if you don't train yourself to mask it. Even when you're not feeling confident, act confidently, and it'll be your fast pass to regaining your confidence quickly.

SELF-COMPASSION FOR YOUR BODY

No one enjoys shaking uncontrollably, having a tight grip, or feeling like they need to vomit. But you don't get to choose how you feel physically. If you did, you'd always feel great. Even if you're fully prepared, the magnitude of the moment can get to you. But you don't need to be a prisoner to how your body feels. Self-compassion can assist you when your body wants to betray you.

Mindfulness helps you experience what you're feeling rather than criticize yourself for feeling that way. Common humanity reminds you that everyone deals with uncomfortable physical sensations. And self-kindness helps you focus on healing the feeling to help you change your perspective from fear to relief.

Revisit the breathing exercises in the Breathing Pillar to get comfortable being with your body and download the breathing audios using the QR code at the beginning of this book. The more comfortable you are being with your breath and your body, the quicker you'll be able to transform your internal environment to meet the external demand.

WHAT YOU IMAGINE, YOUR
BODY MAKES HAPPEN

For good or bad, imagery works. Remember the effect that imagining biting into a lemon had on you? The imagery literally produced physical responses in the form of mini-muscle contractions.

Keep in mind how much your body benefits or is hindered by what you choose to imagine. The more persuaded you are that you can get the job done, the more you train your muscles to fire in your favor.

TRAINING HIGH HEART RATE VARIABILITY (HRV)

Your heart's ability to rise quickly to meet a demand and quickly return to a steady state is known as your heart rate variability (HRV). The higher your HRV, the better you're able to activate your parasympathetic nervous system in charge of calming and soothing you when a stressor subsides. Since sports are both mentally and physically stressful, having a high HRV can be a major benefit. Here are some ways to train your HRV:

- **Physical training.** What kind of physical shape are you in for your sport? Your fitness level will affect your thoughts, emotions, and performance. It's much easier to give in when your throat's on fire and your legs feel like jelly.

  Research shows that good decision-making falls off when your heart rate exceeds 110 beats per minute. The more physically fit you are, the quicker your heart rate drops after meeting a demand, and the better decision-making you'll retain. High-intensity interval training (HIIT) has been shown to be effective in training HRV.

- **Sleep.** Research shows poor sleep quality to be a contributor to low HRV. Some athletes struggle to fall asleep due to stress, while others forego sleep for late-night video game sessions. You should care enough about your career to give your body the rest and recovery it needs. Here are some sleep tips:

  1. Strive for nine hours of sleep per night. Figure out what time you need to wake up and count backward nine-and-a-half hours. For example, if you need to be up at 7:30 in the morning, you should be in bed no later than 10 p.m.

2. Food can impact your digestive system, so don't eat too close to bedtime. Try to go to bed on a near empty stomach.

   Thirty minutes before bedtime, prepare your body for sleep by reading, breathing, or doing visualization. Be as consistent as possible with sleep and rise times. Also, prior to practice or games, try to carve out 20-30 minutes for a power nap for greater clarity and relaxation during your performance.

3. Blackout curtains are ideal when available. If those aren't available, a sleep mask is an affordable alternative. Ear plugs or a white noise machine will block out extra noise. A fan can keep you cool and further block out noise.

4. Temperature: Be sure to sleep in an ideal temperature between sixty to sixty-seven degrees. Use a fan or air conditioner if you have one.

5. Technology: Bright screens decrease the hormones responsible for helping you fall asleep. At least thirty minutes before bed, turn your screens to "Do not disturb" and set them on the other side of the room. This also means you'll have to get out of bed to turn your alarm off in the morning.

- **Nutrition.** Your body is a sports car. Feed it right, and it'll treat you right. Your nutrition is one of the quickest ways to improve your mental and physical state. Take an interest in what you eat and the role good nutrition plays in your performance. You can ask for help from a sports nutritionist or consider buying the following resources to help you figure out the proper proportion of macronutrients (fats, proteins, and carbs) necessary for your body in your specific sport:

  - For youth athletes: *Eat Like a Champion* by Jill Castle
  - For all ages: *Sports Nutrition Guidebook* by Nancy Clark (look for the newest edition)

When athletes eat poorly, they put themselves at risk for nutritional deficiencies and mood swings that'll impact more than their performance. Sleep burns about 50 percent of your calories, which go to rebuilding muscles after exercise, making new tissue, pumping blood throughout the body, and operating the lungs to breathe. The other 50 percent of your calories fuel you for movement and thinking throughout the day.

Hydration is also key to peak performance. Your body is anywhere between 75-85 percent water. Most workouts cause you to lose two pounds of water in sweat. Bring a big jug with you wherever you go. If you're thirsty, you've waited too long. Your urine should be fairly clear throughout the day if you're properly hydrating. Aim for at least 120 ounces of water on practice and game days. If you play in humid climates, drink even more. Dehydration can lead to overheating and injuries. Hydration is one of the easiest ways to improve your performance, so drink up.

The goal of this Body Pillar has been to inform you about the inner workings of your physiology so you can best understand what's going on and not freak out when your body feels hijacked. Remember, you cannot control what your body does, but you are in complete control of how you perceive a situation, which impacts how your body reacts to what's happening.

Strive to be on the attack in the lion mode as much as possible. That way, the body sensations you feel will come from a place of excitement and readiness for the battle ahead.

Pillar 4
BATTLING

17

BATTLING

"I didn't need that extra push to be great, though. From day one, I wanted to dominate. My mindset was: I'm going to figure you out . . . my goal was to figure you out. And to do that, to figure those puzzles out, I was willing to do way more than anyone else. That was the fun part for me."

—Kobe Bryant, NBA basketball great

The combination of your believing, breathing, and body will greatly determine how you battle. There are three main battles you'll face every time you compete or perform:

- me versus me
- me versus you
- me versus the moment

The most important battle is the me-versus-me battle between your ears. This battle is completely in your control. The me-versus-you battle is within your influence. But the me-versus-the-moment battle is out of your control.

Then again, most aspects of your sport will be outside your control. Choose to double down on what's in your control and influence.

ME VERSUS ME

The me-versus-me battle is winnable every time because it's entirely internal. You're usually your toughest opponent and defeat yourself before the opponent gets the chance. Winning the war within starts with your pre-, in-, and post-game routines that will allow you to be single-minded against actual opponents.

PRE-GAME ROUTINES

Sports psychology consultant Brian Cain says, "You don't rise to the occasion. You sink to your preparation." Some athletes show up and see what happens. If you plan on playing at the highest level with any longevity, you can't leave your preparation to chance. Make your pre-game routine a priority and involve both your mind and body. Below is a pre-game visualization you can rehearse to help your mind and body prepare for battle.

◆ **Pre-game visualization.** Speak and record the following script onto your phone using your voice and play it before every practice and game. You may not like the sound of your voice, but when you're out there playing and your voice is all you have to rely on, you'll appreciate having had developed a vocabulary of victory to lead you into battle.

While recording the following, when you see bracketed words like [pause five seconds], keep the recording going, but remain silent for the allotted time before continuing:

Start by getting into a comfortable position and close your eyes [pause ten seconds]. Take a deep breath in through your nose . . . and exhale smoothly through relaxed pursed lips [pause five seconds]. Repeat this breathing pattern a few times, allowing your awareness to fall on the smoothness of the breath [pause thirty seconds].

Now imagine walking toward your mental locker room between red ropes fending off the noisy distractions vying for your attention like the paparazzi. Take a moment and acknowledge them as you walk toward your mental locker room doors [pause ten seconds]. As you approach the doors, your mental security guard opens the door and closes it behind you ... leaving you in peaceful silence in the dim and air-conditioned locker room [pause ten seconds]. As you walk toward your locker, the room gradually lights up, only as much as you want.

At your locker, stare at the full-length mirror until you are convinced the best player in the world is staring back at you. How's your body language? Don't leave the mirror until you're fully convinced that you have what it takes to get the job done today [pause ten seconds]. As you sit down in front of your mirror, it transforms into a TV, displaying your top three favorite highlights. Soak them in. That's you playing at your best. [Pause thirty seconds].

After you've ingrained your highlight reel, see yourself lying on the ground or remaining in your seat. Whatever's most comfortable for you. Begin to inhale powerful words like confidence, boldness, creativity, and love [pause for inhale]. Breathe out weak words like fear, worry, and doubt [pause for exhale]. Breathe in words like strong, assertive, and powerful. Breathe out words like timid, sorry, mistakes, and my bad [pause ten seconds].

Next, is progressive muscle relaxation to check in with each body part combined with compassionate breathing to acknowledge and thank your body for all it does for you. Starting with your toes and working up your body to your head, give each muscle group a gentle squeeze and release while breathing loving-kindness into it. Perhaps, send a soothing emoji face to each muscle before moving on to the next. Now it's your turn [pause two minutes].

Next, visualize yourself playing well [pause 15 seconds]. How do you want to perform today? See yourself dominating and playing the way you know you're capable of [pause thirty seconds].

Now, see yourself struggling [pause ten seconds]. Something will not go your way today. And that's okay. Everything doesn't have to go your way for you to experience success.

As you imagine performing less than ideally, see yourself pausing and recovering with a deep breath, physical touch, and words of encouragement. This can be in a soft tone when you need a hug or a harsh tone when you need a push ... whatever you need in the moment [pause fifteen seconds]. Listen to that inner voice trying to help ... and respond by letting go of what happened and be here now, ready to make the right next move [pause ten seconds].

Just because you struggle at times doesn't make you a bad player. You're just having a down moment like everyone else, and you will recover and get back on track. You'll get back to being the best in the world ... Best in the world ... Best in the world. [Pause ten seconds].

Now, return to your mental locker to notice a piece of paper with "One Day Contract" written at the top with a line at the bottom for you to sign. Pick it up. This is the same contract you must sign every day. Your signature guarantees you'll compete to the best of your abilities in hopes of receiving tomorrow's contract offer. Nothing will be given to you. You must earn it.

After you sign it, set it down and look back in the mirror. All you see is the best in the world. Breathe it in until you believe it in your body [pause ten seconds].

Now . . . all that's left to do is battle. Take one more soothing breath and open your eyes. It's go time.

IN-GAME ROUTINES

The game is constantly changing, but your approach shouldn't. In-game routines provide you with the awareness and focus to confidently perform no matter the moment.

- **Circle of Focus:** On Brian Cain's *Coaching Matters* podcast, a mental performance coach for the Atlanta Braves, Zach Sorenson, shared a story about pitcher Kyle Wright. Kyle had excelled in the minor leagues but couldn't replicate his success at the Major league level. The Braves front office saw Kyle as a heavy contributor at the Major League level and tasked Zach with helping Kyle unlock his potential.

  In their first session, Zach asked Kyle, "When you're on the mound, which circle do you focus on?"

  Kyle was confused.

  Zach followed up with this: "There are two circles on the baseball diamond. Home plate and the pitcher's mound. When you're pitching, where's your focus?"

  "The plate, I guess. That's where all the action happens."

  "Okay. And how much control do you have over what the batter does?"

  "None."

  "What about the catcher?"

  "None."

  "The umpire?"

  "None."

  Zach let that set in. "So, at the Major League level, all your focus flows to home plate where you control absolutely nothing?"

  "Yeah. I guess so."

  "What if you start focusing on the five feet around the mound where you have control until you release the ball?"

Success didn't come right away, but Kyle was able to speed up his learning curve by focusing on the five-foot circle around him instead of trying to control everything else. He eventually became the caliber of pitcher the Braves knew he could be and was a major contributor to the Braves winning the 2021 World Series.

What might happen if you started focusing on the five feet around you rather than everything else? When you get your five feet of focus dialed in, external distractions will still be there, but they'll have to work harder to steal your focus. Within your five feet of focus, own whatever game shows up, whether it's your A, B, or C game.

Treat every playing opportunity like you're bringing your A game, and it might just show up. Either way, within that five-foot bubble, believe whatever you have will get the job done.

◆ **Intention-Attention-Acceptance:** One of the toughest me-versus-me battles is the one for your attention. Our minds are easily distracted. A powerful routine for moving on from whatever happened to be here now is a routine called intention-attention-acceptance.

Intention is what you're setting out to do. *Attention* acts like a spotlight in the dark, shining only on what's important to accomplish your intention. *Acceptance* is your ability to be okay with the results. Acceptance doesn't mean you have to like what happened; it just means you aren't ruminating about how you wish things were different.

Acceptance is for humans like you and me who don't always perform perfectly. The quicker you accept whatever happens, the better you set yourself up for your next opportunity. Let's use one of my practice range sessions at the golf course to help bring this routine to life.

◆ **Intent:** I pull out my 7-iron, bring my eyes to the 175-yard flag, and stay there until my mind relays to my body what I want it to do. While my eyes are glued to the flag, I use third-person visualization to step out of my body and see my desired swing path and follow-through.

Then I visualize the flight of the ball as it gets pulled toward the flag with a magnetic force. The imagery isn't perfect. It's fragmented at best. But vividness isn't a requirement for effectiveness.

◆ **Attention:** After I'm fully persuaded about my intent, I bring my eyes to the golf ball like a spotlight but with a soft focus that's almost blurry. Without moving my club, I imagine my club head going back and coming through, creating a video game-like explosion at impact. Then, in real life, I inhale as my club head goes back and I sharpen my focus on one dimple of the golf ball and say, "Explode." On my exhale my club head comes down and strikes the ball. The trigger word "explode" reminds my eyes to stay at the point of impact after my swing finishes.

◆ **Acceptance:** After impact, I get a sense of the flight of the ball. Sometimes the ball does exactly what I want it to do, and sometimes it doesn't. When it doesn't, I have two choices: resist what's happening or accept it. No matter what, I cannot change what happens. So I must accept it. I train my mind to accept the result by:

> ◆ Separating myself from my performance.
>
> ◆ Allowing whatever I feel to be there without over-identifying with the feelings.
>
> ◆ Allowing room for failure because I know how challenging the game is.
>
> ◆ Learning from what happened.
>
> ◆ Resetting with new intent.

Each phase of the intention-attention-acceptance routine is the most critical phase while you're in it. Give persistent attention to precisely what you're doing. Then, accept what happens so you can reset your intention for the next moment without emotional attachment.

Acceptance gets easier and less personal. The more you understand you can't change what is, the less time you'll waste wishing things were different. As you work toward intention-attention-acceptance routine mastery, you'll get better at funneling your focus for one specific moment at a time. There will soon be little to no emotional attachment to whatever happens. All that will be left is a quiet mind for you to trust your skills.

POST-GAME ROUTINES

Most athletes chalk their performances up to being good or bad without mining them for every ounce of gold. Others stew for hours or days over what went wrong. But that's not the way to show you care. If you expect to improve, a post-game evaluation routine will help you break down exactly what happened so you can grow and move forward. How much value are you leaving by not systematically evaluating how you played? Measurement reignites motivation. After games, ask yourself what went well, what could've gone better, and how you'll improve moving forward.

Your post-game evaluation should actually start *before* the game. Write out your process goals that will lead to success and that you'll evaluate post-game. Process goals should be measurable actions that relate to the end goal. For instance, first-pitch strike percentage in baseball or softball is a measurable process goal. Why would you want to throw a first-pitch strike? Because percentages show getting ahead in the count leads to more outs and fewer pitches thrown (a great end goal). After the game, instead of focusing on the score, you can evaluate how well you accomplished your goal of throwing first-pitch strikes.

Evaluate your performance based on your process goals rather than results. Too many things outside your control influence your chances of success. Process goals can be mental or physical. A mental process goal might be: how quickly did I have emotional awareness when adversity struck? Keep track of your mental and physical process goals in a notebook for several games and see how your performance changes when focusing on measurables.

- ◆ **Strive for five.** A simple tool for evaluating performance rationally rather than emotionally is rating yourself on a scale of 1-5, 1 being terrible, 5 being better than ever. Giving yourself a number grade keeps the emotions out of it and allows you to be honest with yourself without judgment. "Strive for five" can also be used as an in-game routine between plays or pitches to evaluate anything mental or physical. My baseball clients use it to assess how well they caught the ball in the palm (infielders), how well they hit a spot (pitchers), or how close to the sweet spot they hit the ball (batters).

Failing to set pre-game goals leads to aimlessness during games and gives you no criteria for improvement after the game. You'll still feel something about the way you played but will be without a map to make sense of it. This leads to internalizing your performance and blaming yourself or others for the outcome.

Regret is a common feeling among athletes after games. Although regret is considered something you don't want to live with, I challenge that idea. Regret is incredibly valuable if used correctly. Regret informs you that you could've done something better. Without regret, we wouldn't strive to do better next time.

So, when you feel regret, listen to it. It'll point you exactly to where you know you can do better next time. Live with regrets. Learn from them. Then let them go and focus on what's next.

ME VERSUS YOU

Once you've won the battle of me versus me, you're ready to focus on the me-versus-you battle with your actual opponent. Every comic book superhero has a villain who brings out the best in them. Magic had Bird. Jordan had the Pistons. Tom Brady had the Manning brothers. Good opponents will demand your all. Welcome the challenge.

MAKE IT PERSONAL

Before Game 1 of a playoff series, Michael Jordan would often walk into the opposing team's locker room to shake hands and welcome them to Chicago. In reality, he didn't care to shake hands. He wanted them to think more about him than about what they needed to do to beat him. Michael was one of the best at making the me-versus-you battle personal. He was an assassin on the court, and it didn't take much for a player to get on his hit list.

On a 1993 night in the Windy City, Jordan had one of his worst games while a young LaBradford Smith of the Washington Bullets had the game of his life, scoring thirty-seven points. After the game, Smith and Jordan crossed paths on the way to the locker room. Smith put his arm around Michael and uttered, "Nice game, Mike."

Those three simple words woke a sleeping dog. The next night, the Bulls and Bullets were scheduled to square off again, but this time the game would be in Washington. On the flight, Jordan told teammates, "Tomorrow, in the first half, I'm going to have what this kid had in the entire game."

Jordan proceeded to score thirty-six points in the first half, a point short of his promise, but he sure got Smith's attention. Bulls teammate B.J. Armstrong said about Jordan's night, "I never seen a man go after another player the way he did."

Michael Jordan used a harmless post-game comment as fuel to torch Smith on his own court. That's making it personal.

The crazy part? Decades later, rumors spread that the "Nice game, Mike" encounter never happened. When reporters asked Jordan about it, he smiled and said he'd made the whole thing up, but there's enough evidence that His Airness used grudges and even made up scenarios to fuel himself to victory. Nothing was off limits in getting him to the mental space to beat his opponent.

The best are willing to do what it takes mentally and physically to prepare themselves to win because they understand losing is a very real possibility. Your opponent has one job: to stop you from getting what you want. Your opponent is like a thief in the night trying to break into your home to steal what's yours. Your thought process should go like this: *Step into my house, and it's not going to go well for you.*

Now it's personal. Knowing that losing is a possibility creates a heightened awareness and sense of urgency from the get-go. Although losing is always possible, there's no need to dwell on it. Keep your focus on doing what needs to be done now to win. Don't get frantic when you fall behind. It's part of the game. Remember, the other team is human, too, so play to the finish. Play to win. And make it personal.

STICK TO YOUR STRENGTHS

On July 7, 2022, Boston Red Sox slugger Rafael Devers hit two home runs off New York Yankees ace pitcher Gerrit Cole at Yankee Stadium. Prior to that game, Devers had already homered four times off Cole. He had Cole's number, and they both knew it. To right the ship, Cole began changing up his game plan completely whenever the two squared off. Instead of using his dominant fastball, Cole threw Devers a steady diet of off-speed pitches, which Devers hit hard anyway. The consensus was that the Yankees couldn't figure out how to get Devers out.

Fast forward ten days to July 17, back at Yankee Stadium, where Cole and Devers faced off again. This time, Cole returned to the strengths that annually made him a Cy Young Award candidate. He attacked Devers with fastballs averaging 98 miles-per-hour all over the zone. The result? Two strikeouts and a weak pop-up.

The takeaway? Play to your strengths rather than overthink things. When Gerrit Cole played to his strengths—his fastballs—he got the desired results. You have to believe your best stuff will get the job done. If it doesn't, tip your cap to your opponent as the better player that day and hope to have another chance against them down the road.

ME VERSUS THE MOMENT

Athletes see the game through their own perspective. Do you see your performance as life or death? Or as a game where risk-taking, triumph, and heartache only exist between the lines? You can't control most situations you'll encounter throughout a game, but you can control your perspective toward what's happening in front of you.

THE SPORTS ILLUSION

Your sport will paint the illusion that it's the most important thing in the world, but it's not. All the emotional strings sports pull are only as real as you want to make them. Your sport doesn't put pressure on you. You put pressure on yourself based on the meaning you give a situation.

Ask yourself, "Is this moment *really* worth stressing over?" Maybe it is. But that decision should at least be yours to make. You play sports to escape the pressures of real life and have fun. Yet, many athletes and weekend warriors find a way to make their athletic careers more stressful than real life.

Sports are similar to the game of Monopoly, where you roll the dice and go around the board with momentary ups and downs. Someone wins. Everyone else loses. Emotions fly. Friendships are tested. The better you grasp that your sport isn't life or death, the freer you'll be to compete like crazy and embrace every up and down that comes your way—knowing life will go on afterward. This isn't the *Hunger Games.*

Sports are a low-risk, high-reward environment that affords you the freedom to feel all the feels, knowing it's not real life. Your troubles only exist within the confines of the game, so enjoy the built-in frustration and exhilaration. The second a game stops being fun and becomes too real, it loses its benefits.

You choose to play your sport because you enjoy it. If you don't enjoy it, don't play. Sports are a game for entertainment, no matter what anyone tells you. Having the proper perspective doesn't make you less competitive. It may actually give you the competitive edge over someone who views sports as life or death.

THE SIMPLICITY BATTLE

In the fall of 2021, I met with a Division 1 baseball player named Ryan to discuss what success looked like going into his first draft-eligible season in 2022. Ryan said, "Last year during Covid, we only played a handful of games, so my goal was to go one-for-three with a walk every game. It was stressful, but I dang near hit that goal."

Sports are only as stressful as you make them. They're even more stressful when you focus on results instead of the processes to get those results. For 2022, Ryan's results goals were: to make All-Conference again, be a team leader, get drafted in the top four rounds, and have an OPS (on-base percentage plus slugging) of 1.000. Lofty goals but doable in his eyes.

Two months into the season, Ryan was having his worst year of baseball. If he hoped to get drafted at all, he needed to shed every mental brick holding him back. I asked him to be willing to throw out everything to simplify hitting down to the bare elements. After some thought, Ryan smiled during our FaceTime call and made a new goal: "Hit the ball hard or find a way to get on base."

Bingo. By simplifying his approach, Ryan climbed out of the hole he'd dug for himself. In doing so, he kept his hope alive that his wildest dreams could still come true. Once he shed all the expectations and started competing one pitch at a time, Ryan salvaged his season and ended up hitting .300. And yes, he got drafted.

Many athletes get caught up in the flashy rewards dangling in front of them or the magnitude of what they think is a "big game." Yet, these are like fake lures set to catch fish. Don't fall for them. Keep things as simple as possible and keep your mind on the day-to-day steps that will get you closer to your end goal. For Ryan, his self-imposed expectations weren't allowing him to execute the simple tasks of seeing the ball well and hitting it hard. What complicates your simple? Start simple. Stay simple.

IF-THEN STATEMENTS

Let's face it: sports can wreak havoc on your emotions because your sport means so much to you. To react emotionally when things don't go your way is okay because you're going to feel those feelings anyways. But to overreact out of habit or as a demonstration of how much you care is unnecessary. It'll only get you closer to being on tilt and farther away from being on track. Being on tilt is a state of being emotionally out of control after a mistake that causes you to play recklessly to make up for what happened. News flash: You can't make up for what happened. It already happened. You can only position your mind and body to be effective now.

Every sport has their own version of tilting. Fouling a player who fouled you or yelling at an official after a questionable call can seem like a reasonable reaction or even the right thing to do in the heat of the moment. But it never is. So, how does one overcome the urge to tilt and stay emotionally balanced?

Prior to competition, develop an "if-then" list to fireproof your decision-making, no matter what emotional state you're in. Having a pre-determined plan takes the guesswork out of in-the-moment decision-making and stops you from doing something you'll likely soon regret. An if-then statement gives you the power of hindsight before you need it.

If-then lists are only helpful if you have the awareness to use them. Sometimes emotions spike so quickly you react before pausing to think. To combat this, practice visualizing your if-then statements in situations where you become emotionally out of control. When you practice in advance how you would like to respond to whatever happens, the planned response will become more natural and save you further pain.

On Grant Parr's *90% Mental* podcast, Thane Ringler, a former professional golfer, shared how he dealt with highly emotional moments during competition. "No matter how great you are, you're going to have terrible shots or off days," Ringler said. "In these moments, I would reframe and rename my shots. I'd say, 'I wasn't planning on hitting into the trees today, but it looks like a great opportunity to get creative.'"

Reframing and renaming his situation allowed Ringler to have fun with his next shot rather than feel the need to make up for his screw-up. He had to remember that one poor shot didn't have to determine his day.

Ringler's reframe and rename technique was something he built into his game plan so that no matter what happened, he had something to go to when he needed it. What do you go to when you need it? If you're not prepared, your emotions will guide your performance. Make an if-then statement list to help you navigate tense moments.

Remember, when it comes to battling, you control very little. Double down on what's in your control and remember your opponent is human and liable to make mistakes. They have to win the internal war before they ever battle you.

The more you win the me-versus-me battle, the better chance you'll have of bringing your best versus your opponent and the moment.

SOME FINAL THOUGHTS . . .

So, there you have it—my long-winded answer to the question, "When an athlete comes to you for help, what's your approach?"

The Pillar B framework is that approach, and these principles will help you believe in yourself one play at a time.

Remember, anyone can believe, breathe, be aware of his or her body, and battle for one play. But mastery comes when you can tap into your Pillar B's every play.

You are now equipped to be your own best coach. All that's left to do is put the Pillar B's into play. Here's one final review:

PILLAR 1: BELIEVING: YOUR FIVE KEYS TO CONFIDENCE

◆ **Perspective.** Believe you're the best athlete to get the job done at this moment, no matter how you've played.

◆ **Identity.** If you plan to get where you want to go, decide who you are, why you *really* play, and how you'll navigate the pleasures and pressures ready to detour your career.

◆ **Self-Compassion.** Failure will cause you to be your biggest critic, but with self-compassion, you become your best coach through mindfulness, common humanity, and self-kindness.

◆ **Vocabulary of Victory.** There's constant conflict waging between your ears, but a vocabulary of victory guarantees winning the war within.

◆ **Vision.** Your mind is happy to turn toward Negative Town, but when you consistently imagine the future you desire—whether it's the next play or the next thirty years—you give yourself concrete evidence to strive toward.

PILLAR 2: BREATHING: YOUR TWO KEYS TO EMOTIONAL ACCOUNTABILITY

◆ **A Gauge . . . Not a Guide.** Your emotions will guide you, or you can use them to gauge your feelings and how much a moment means to you.

◆ **Emotion Regulation Systems.** Threat, drive, and soothe systems each have value. Train yourself to tap into the right one at the right time. Your breath is a superpower . . . treat it as such.

PILLAR 3: BODY: YOUR TWO KEYS TO AN OPTIMAL BODY STATE

◆ **The Gazelle, Lion, or Mother Bear Modes.** At times you'll feel like a gazelle, but in sports, only the lion or mother bear modes will prevail.

◆ **Body Language.** Sometimes you won't have it in you to conjure up confidence from within, so you'll need to manufacture it from the outside in.

PILLAR 4: BATTLING: YOUR THREE KEY BATTLES

- **Me Versus Me.** Internal doubts and distractions will sometimes be there, but you can funnel your focus with your pre-game, in-game, and post-game routines.

- **Me Versus You.** Their job is to stop you from getting what you want, but you've never been more ready to get what's yours. Control your five feet of focus.

- **Me Versus the Moment.** You can't control the moment, but you can control how you see it.

Background noise will always be there.

Despite it . . .

Believe you're the best in this moment.

Breathe in the present moment.

Be aware of your body in the moment.

Battle the correct opponent in the moment.

These pillars are your strong foundation that'll help you weather anything.

I see the storms coming.

Will you still be standing?

I'm confident you will be

If you enjoyed this book, would you take
a moment to review it on amazon.com
and share your biggest takeaways?

Want to join a community of likeminded athletes striving to become more? Consider joining the Pillar B's Academy where you'll get access to:

- ◆ Weekly Group Accountability ZOOM Sessions
- ◆ Monthly Challenges
- ◆ In-Depth Courses covering each of the Pillar B's
- ◆ And much more . .

Visit: ThePillarBsAcademy.com

CONNECT WITH RAY ON SOCIAL MEDIA:

f RenewedMindPerformance

🐦 RenewedMindRay

📷 RenewedMindPerformance

Lightning Source UK Ltd.
Milton Keynes UK
UKHW022313070223
416656UK00022B/260